The Climate Crisis

FOSSIL FUELS

A Graphic Guide

Stephanie Loureiro
illustrated by Julie Lerche

Graphic Universe™ • Minneapolis

Graphic Universe™
An imprint of Lerner Publishing Group, Inc.
241 First Avenue North
Minneapolis, MN 55401 USA

For reading levels and more information, look up this title at www.lernerbooks.com.

Main body text is set in Dave Gibbons Lower. Typeface provided by Comicraft.

Library of Congress Cataloging-in-Publication Data

Names: Loureiro, Stephanie, author. | Lerche, Julie, illustrator.
Title: Fossil fuels : a graphic guide / written by Stephanie Loureiro ; illustrated by Julie Lerche.
Description: Minneapolis : Graphic Universe, [2023] | Series: The climate crisis | Includes bibliographical references and index. | Audience: Ages 8–12 | Audience: Grades 4–6 | Summary: "Fossil fuels heat homes and power vehicles. But every use of these fuels adds to rising temperatures on Earth. Examine how fossil fuels have been used and the effect they have on our planet's climate"— Provided by publisher.
Identifiers: LCCN 2023010109 (print) | LCCN 2023010110 (ebook) | ISBN 9781728476896 (library binding) | ISBN 9798765623503 (paperback) | ISBN 9798765613221 (epub)
Subjects: LCSH: Fossil fuels—Juvenile literature. | Climate change—Juvenile literature. | Graphic novels. | BISAC: JUVENILE NONFICTION / Science & Nature / Earth Sciences / General
Classification: LCC TP318.3 .L68 2023 (print) | LCC TP318.3 (ebook) | DDC 662.6—dc23/eng/20230328

LC record available at https://lccn.loc.gov/2023010109
LC ebook record available at https://lccn.loc.gov/2023010110

Manufactured in the United States of America
1 – CG – 7/15/23

TABLE OF CONTENTS

Chapter One: What Are Fossil Fuels?

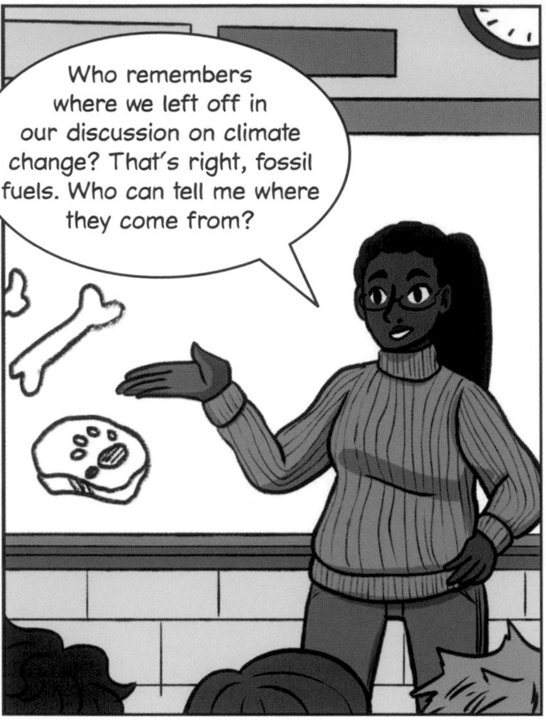
Who remembers where we left off in our discussion on climate change? That's right, fossil fuels. Who can tell me where they come from?

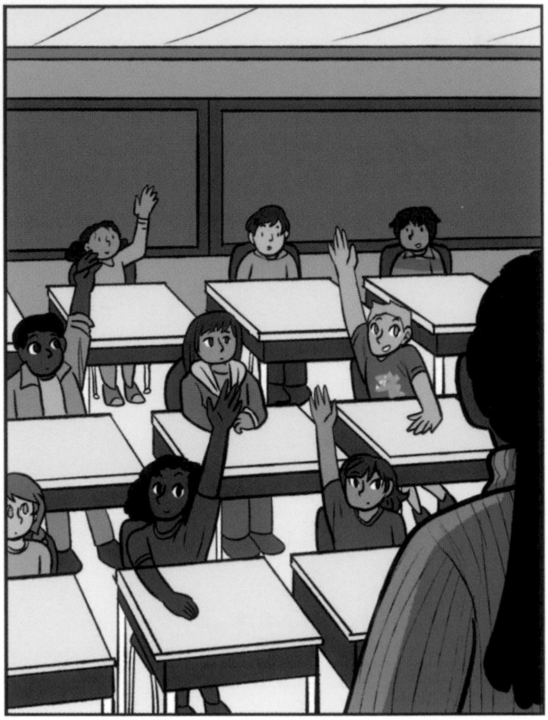

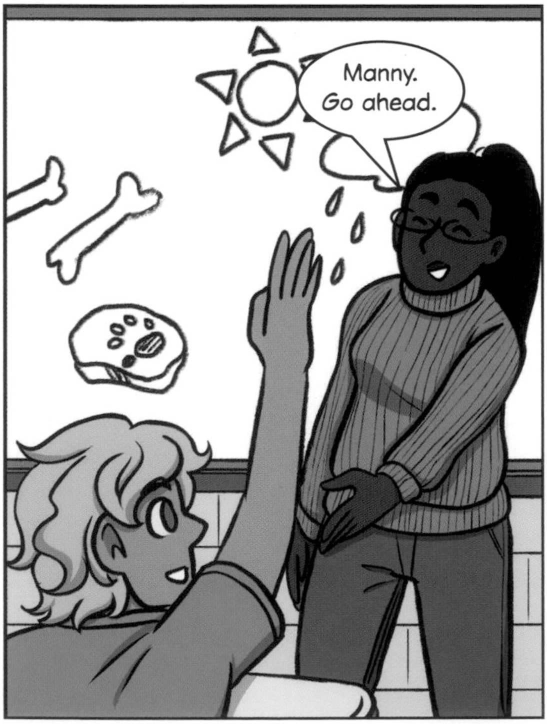
Manny. Go ahead.

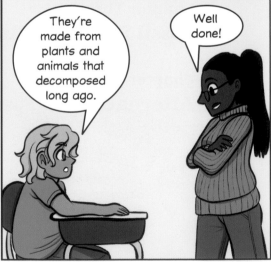

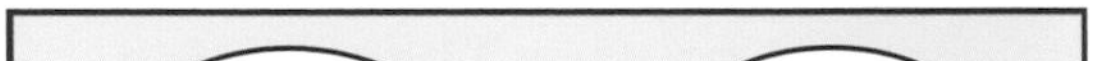
They're made from plants and animals that decomposed long ago.
Well done!

Fossil fuels develop deep underground—about 200 to 300 feet below the surface*. They can take millions of years to form. In fact, the coal people use formed about 300 million years ago.

*61 to 91 meters

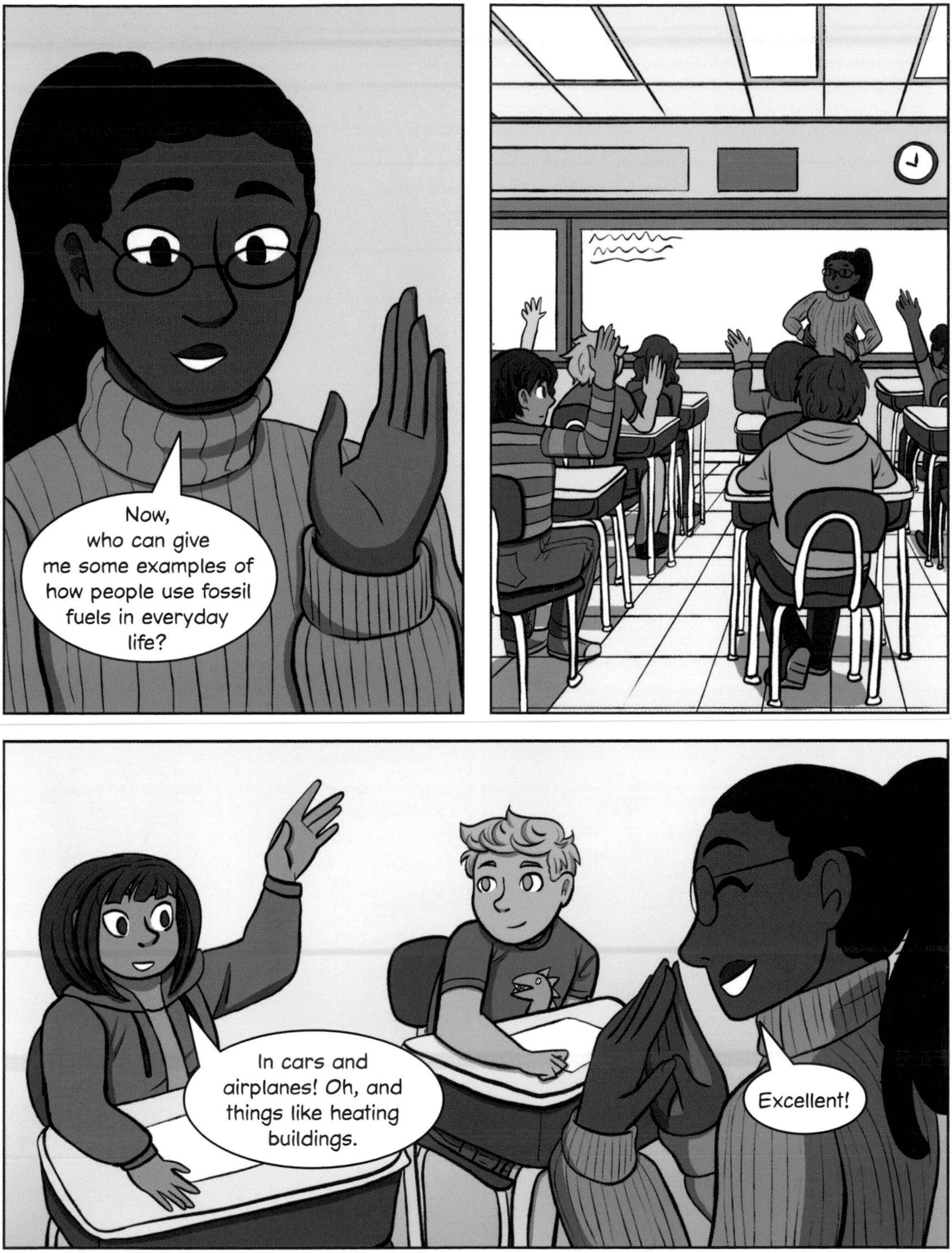
Now, who can give me some examples of how people use fossil fuels in everyday life?
In cars and airplanes! Oh, and things like heating buildings.
Excellent!

Fossil fuels are the main source of energy in countries around the world, including the United States. But they aren't found everywhere. About half of the world's oil supply is in the Middle East.

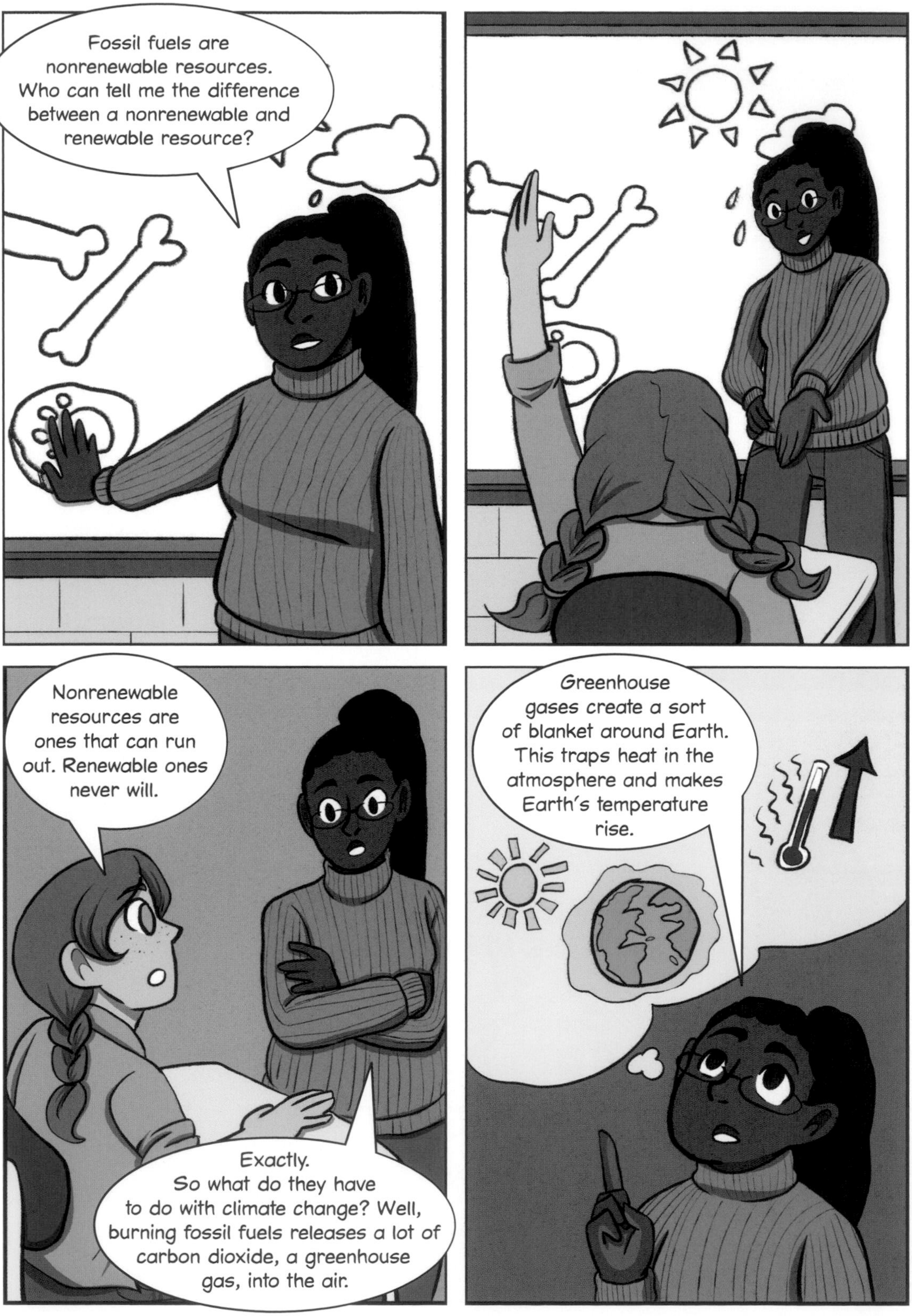
Fossil fuels are nonrenewable resources. Who can tell me the difference between a nonrenewable and renewable resource?
Nonrenewable resources are ones that can run out. Renewable ones never will.
Exactly. So what do they have to do with climate change? Well, burning fossil fuels releases a lot of carbon dioxide, a greenhouse gas, into the air.
Greenhouse gases create a sort of blanket around Earth. This traps heat in the atmosphere and makes Earth's temperature rise.

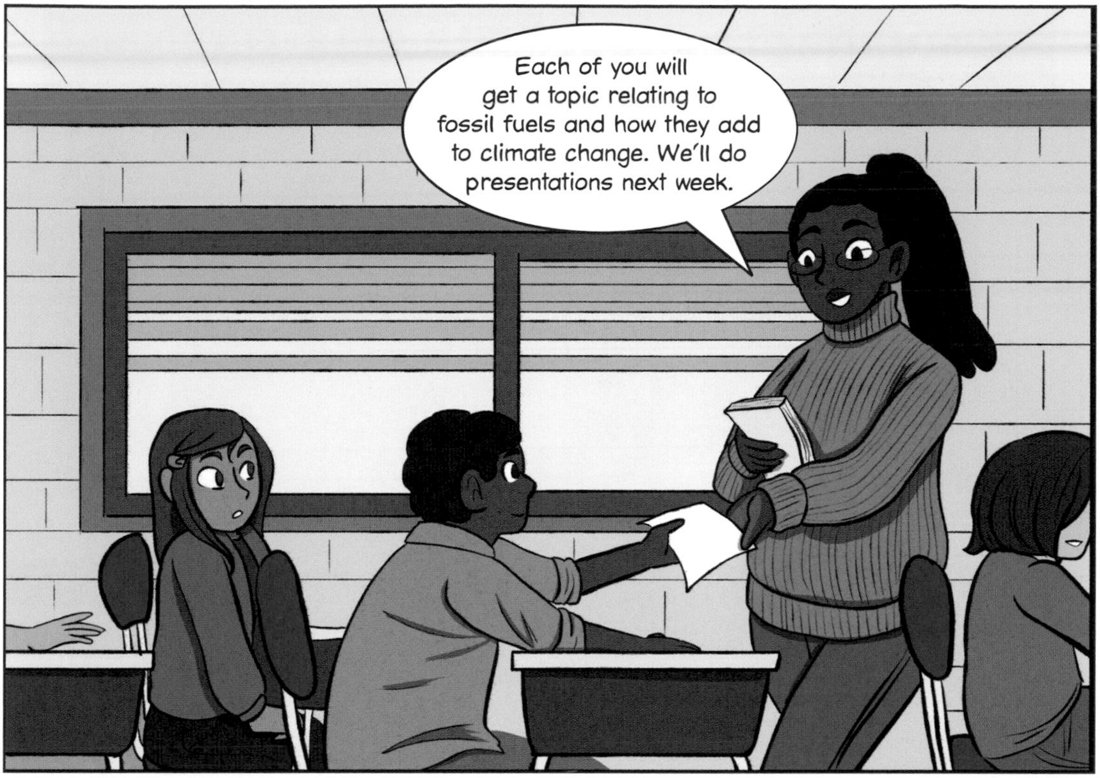
Each of you will get a topic relating to fossil fuels and how they add to climate change. We'll do presentations next week.

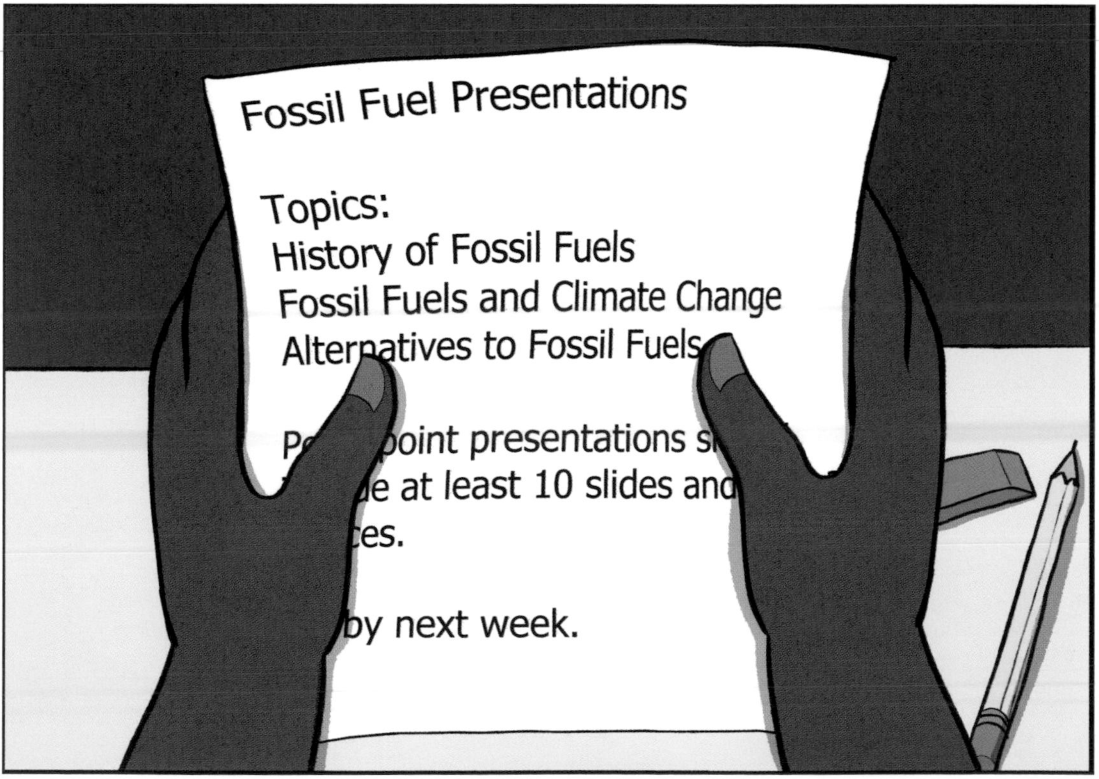
Fossil Fuel Presentations
Topics:
History of Fossil Fuels
Fossil Fuels and Climate Change
Alternatives to Fossil Fuels
point presentations s
de at least 10 slides and
ces.
by next week.

Chapter Two: Fossil Fuel Usage

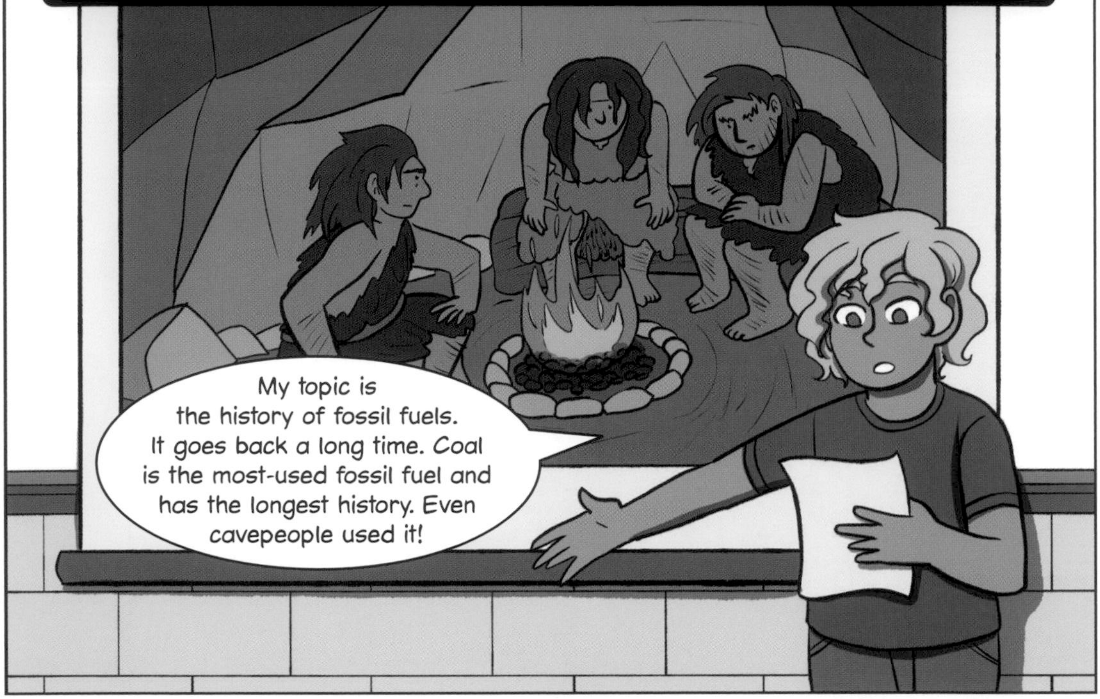
My topic is the history of fossil fuels. It goes back a long time. Coal is the most-used fossil fuel and has the longest history. Even cavepeople used it!

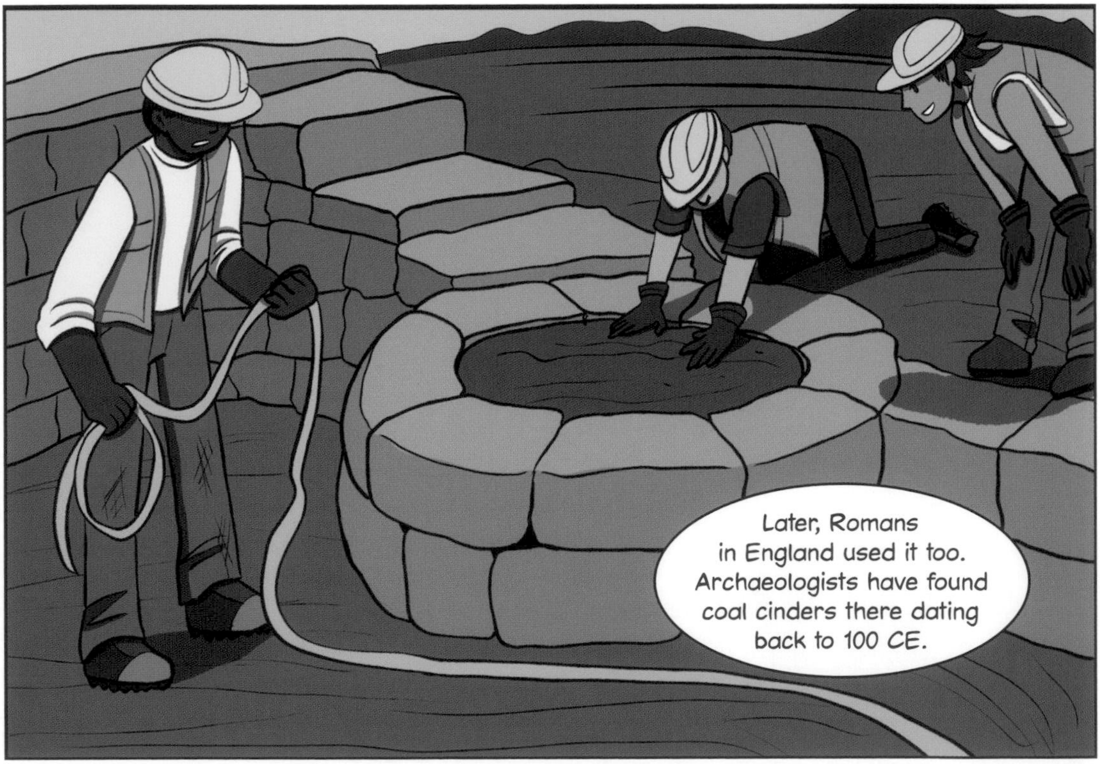
Later, Romans in England used it too. Archaeologists have found coal cinders there dating back to 100 CE.

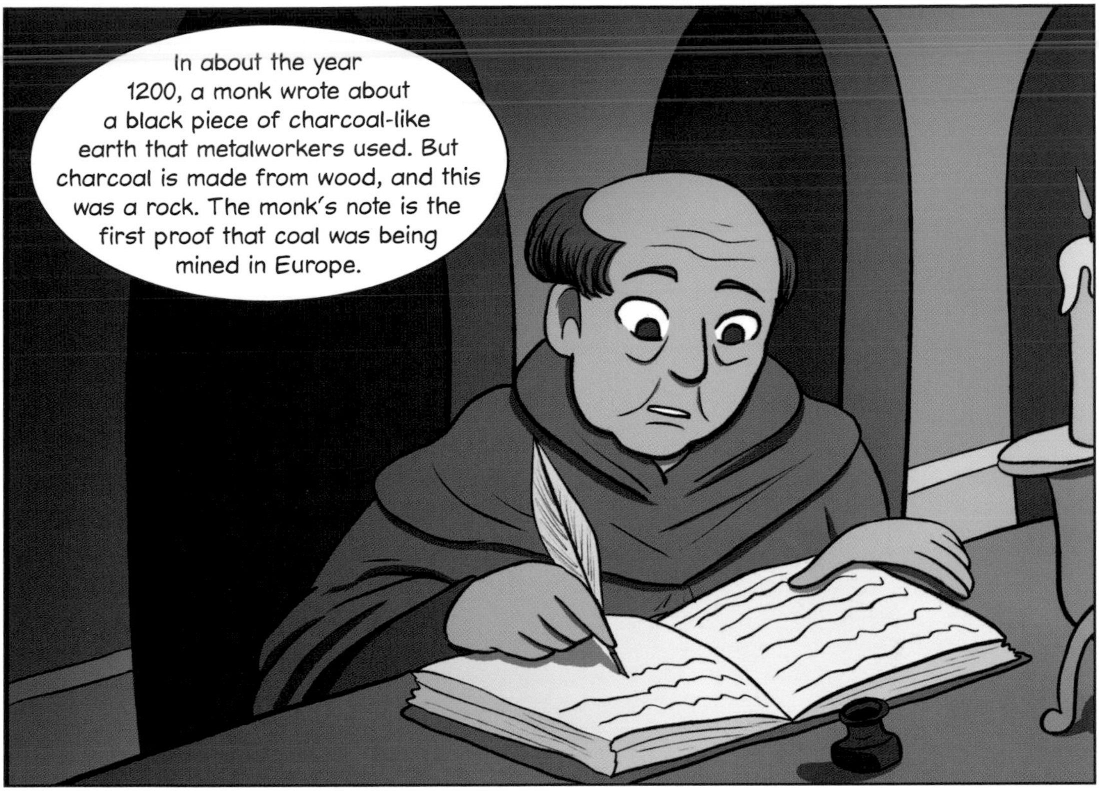
In about the year 1200, a monk wrote about a black piece of charcoal-like earth that metalworkers used. But charcoal is made from wood, and this was a rock. The monk's note is the first proof that coal was being mined in Europe.

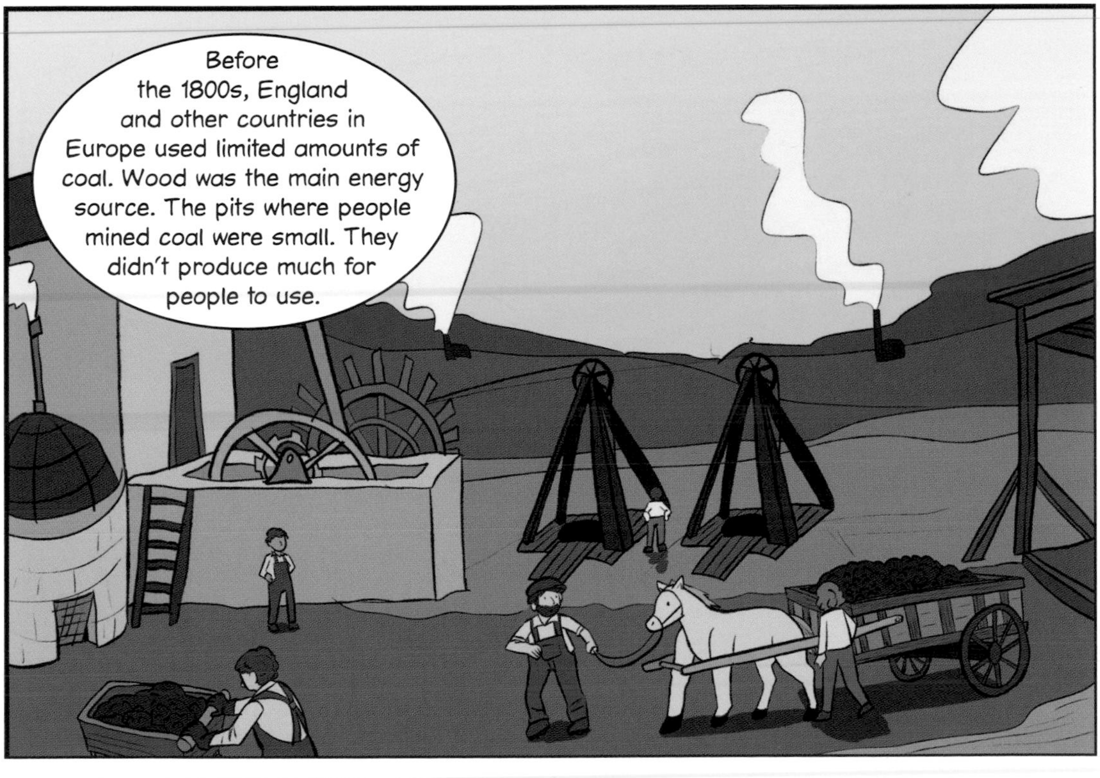
Before the 1800s, England and other countries in Europe used limited amounts of coal. Wood was the main energy source. The pits where people mined coal were small. They didn't produce much for people to use.

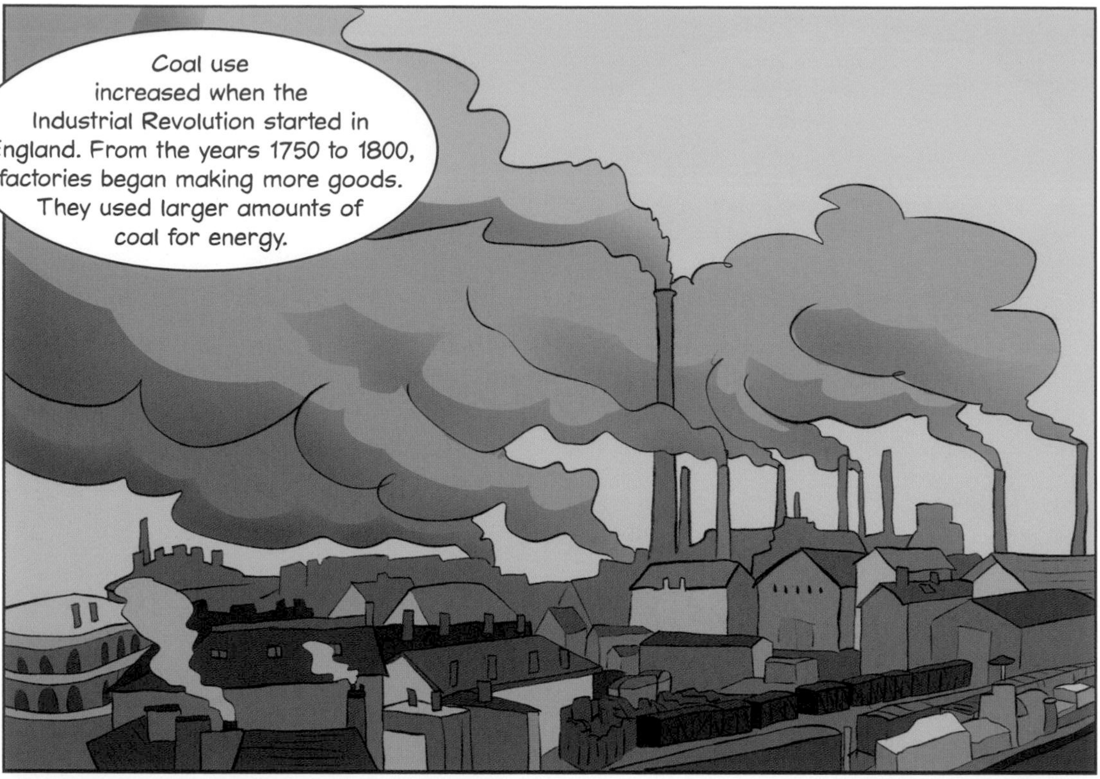
Coal use increased when the Industrial Revolution started in England. From the years 1750 to 1800, factories began making more goods. They used larger amounts of coal for energy.

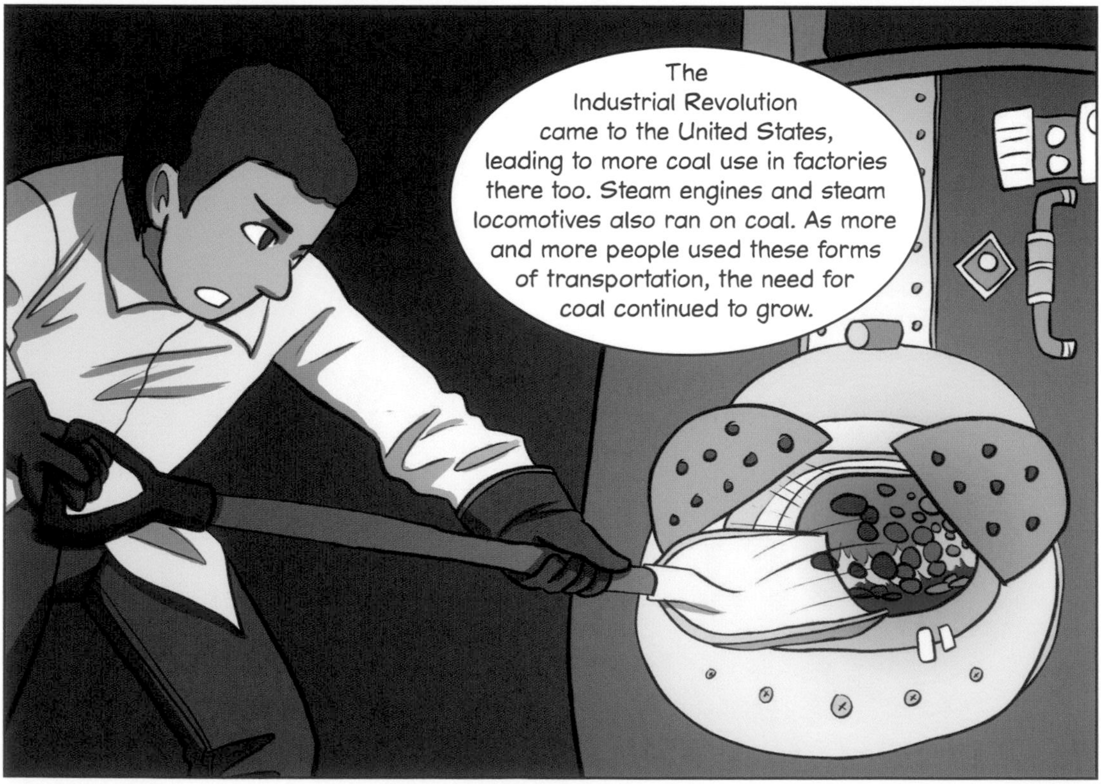
The Industrial Revolution came to the United States, leading to more coal use in factories there too. Steam engines and steam locomotives also ran on coal. As more and more people used these forms of transportation, the need for coal continued to grow.

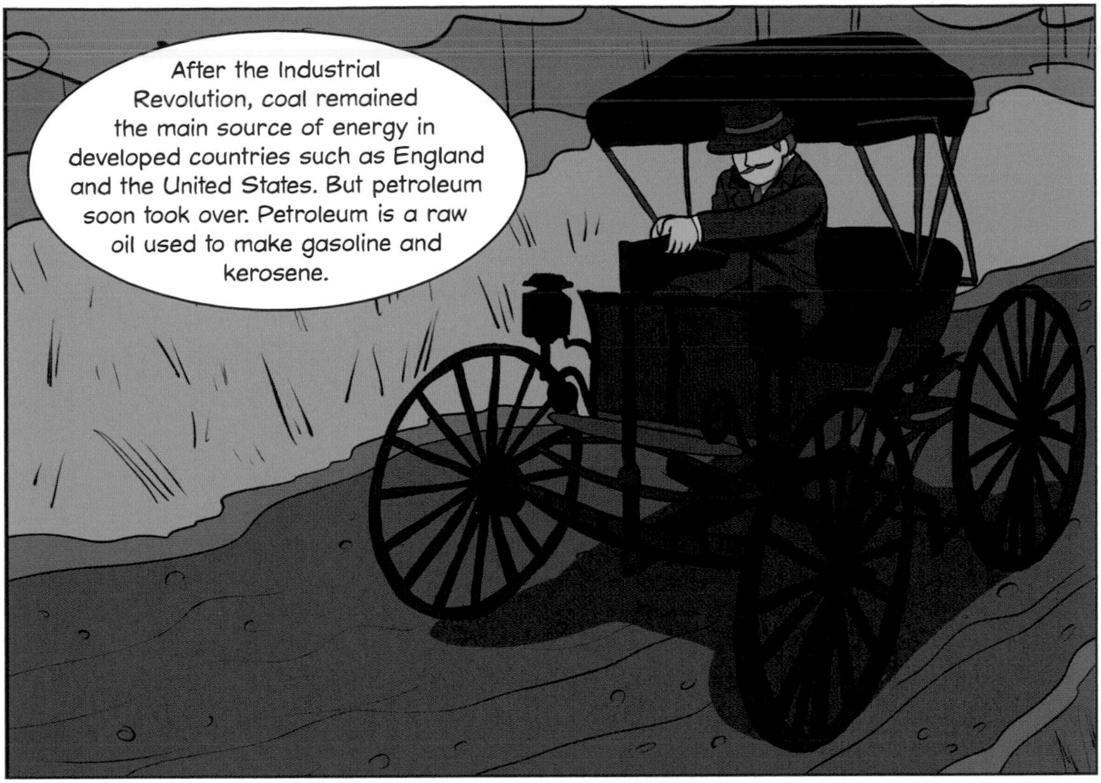
After the Industrial Revolution, coal remained the main source of energy in developed countries such as England and the United States. But petroleum soon took over. Petroleum is a raw oil used to make gasoline and kerosene.

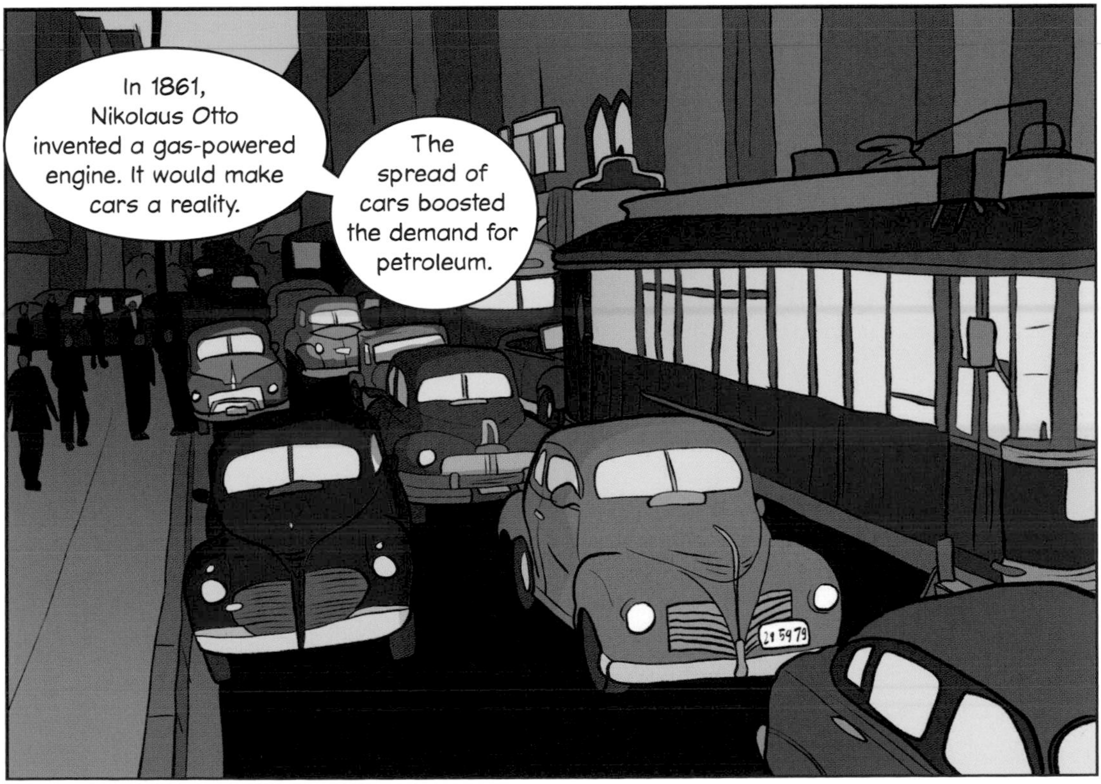
In 1861, Nikolaus Otto invented a gas-powered engine. It would make cars a reality.
The spread of cars boosted the demand for petroleum.

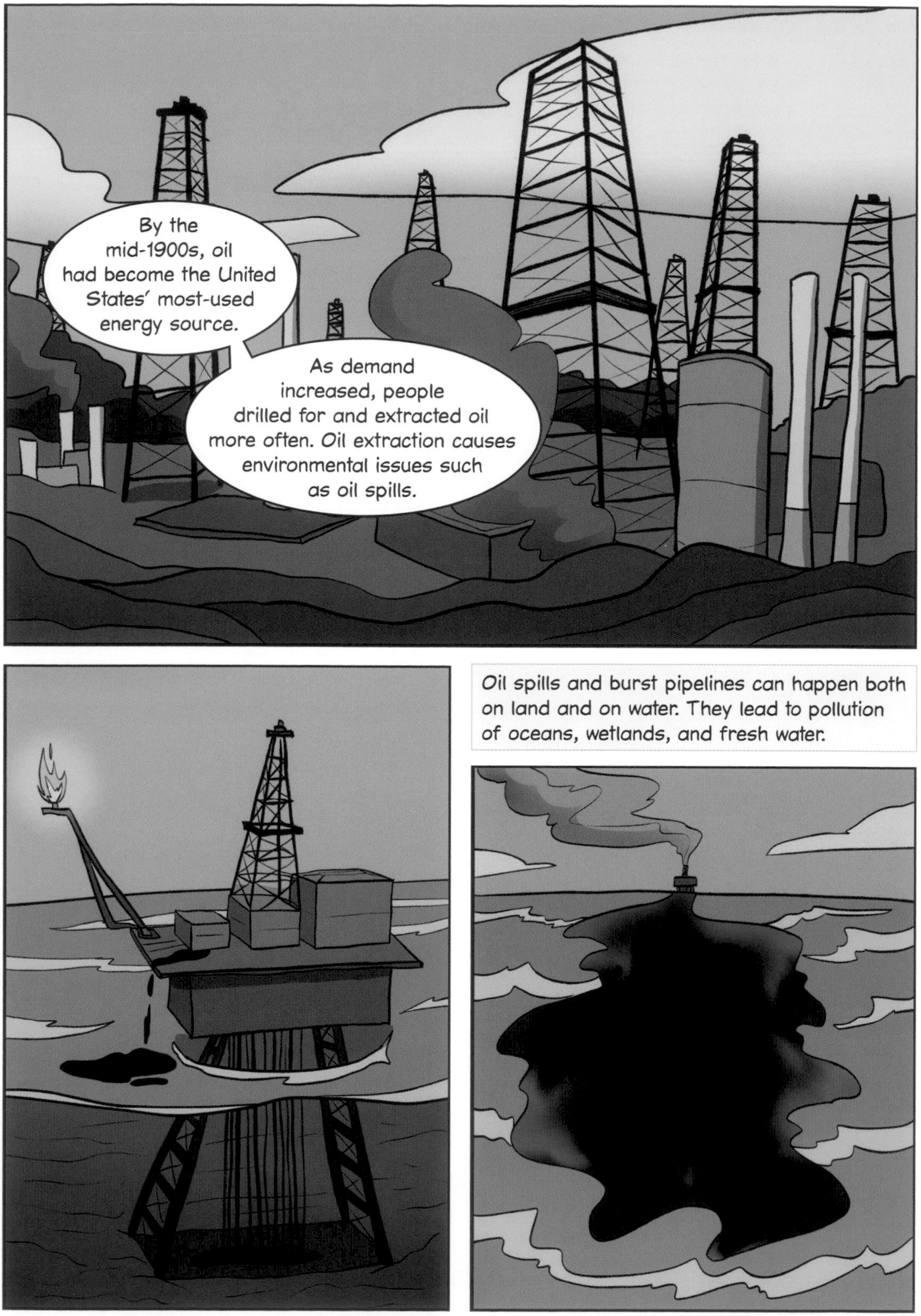
By the mid-1900s, oil had become the United States' most-used energy source.
As demand increased, people drilled for and extracted oil more often. Oil extraction causes environmental issues such as oil spills.
Oil spills and burst pipelines can happen both on land and on water. They lead to pollution of oceans, wetlands, and fresh water.

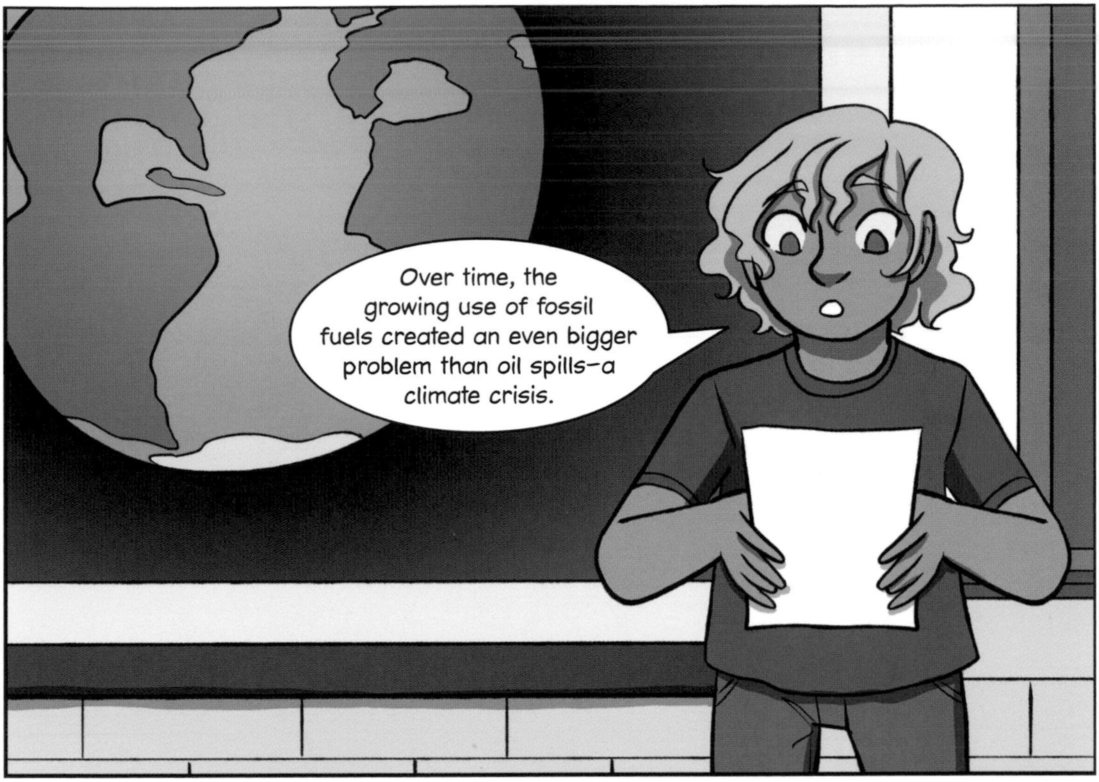
Over time, the growing use of fossil fuels created an even bigger problem than oil spills—a climate crisis.

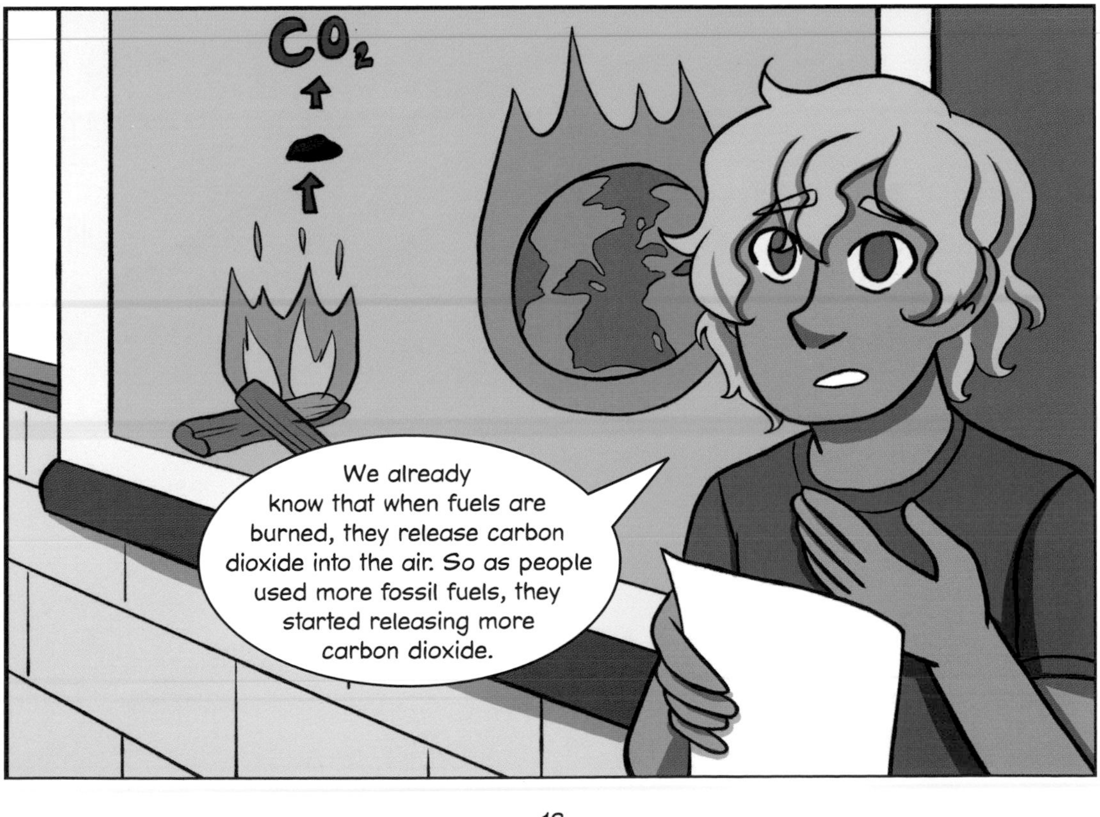
CO_2
We already know that when fuels are burned, they release carbon dioxide into the air. So as people used more fossil fuels, they started releasing more carbon dioxide.

Chapter Three: Fossil Fuels and Climate Change

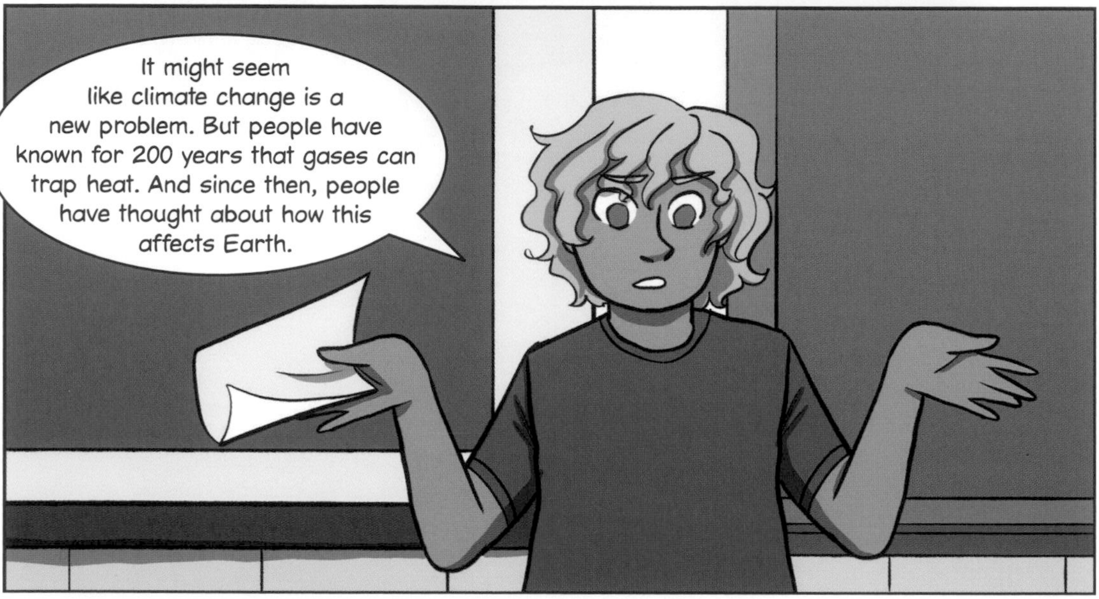
It might seem like climate change is a new problem. But people have known for 200 years that gases can trap heat. And since then, people have thought about how this affects Earth.

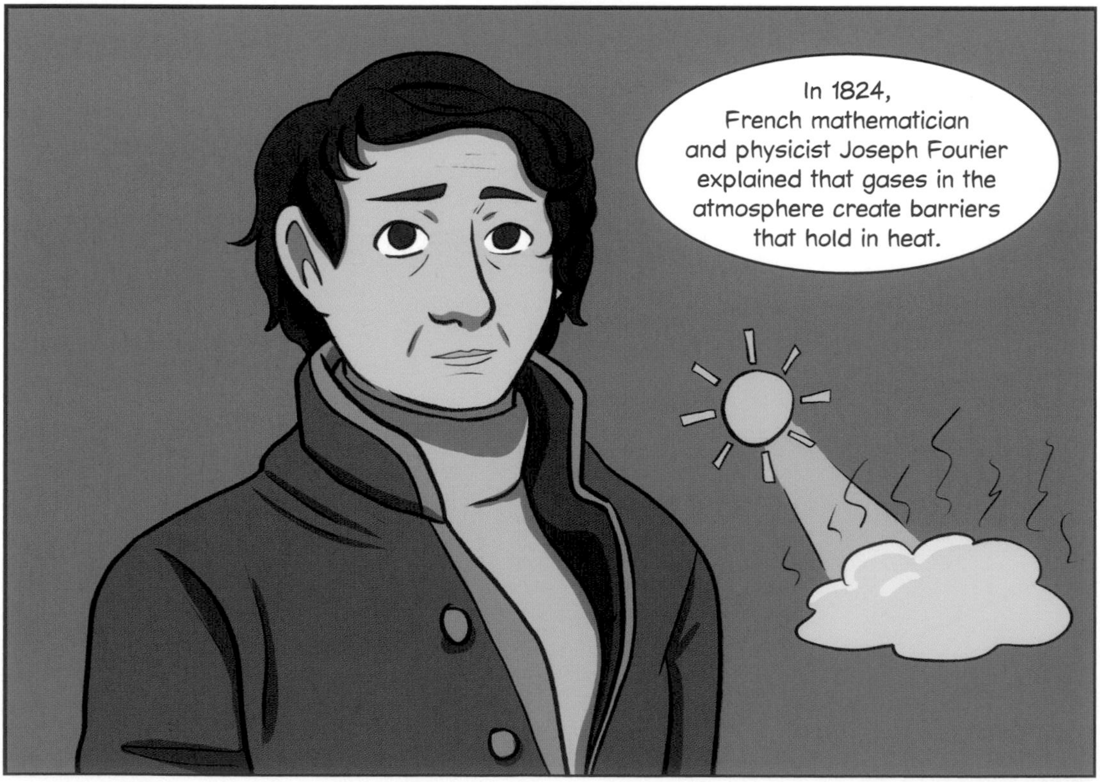
In 1824, French mathematician and physicist Joseph Fourier explained that gases in the atmosphere create barriers that hold in heat.

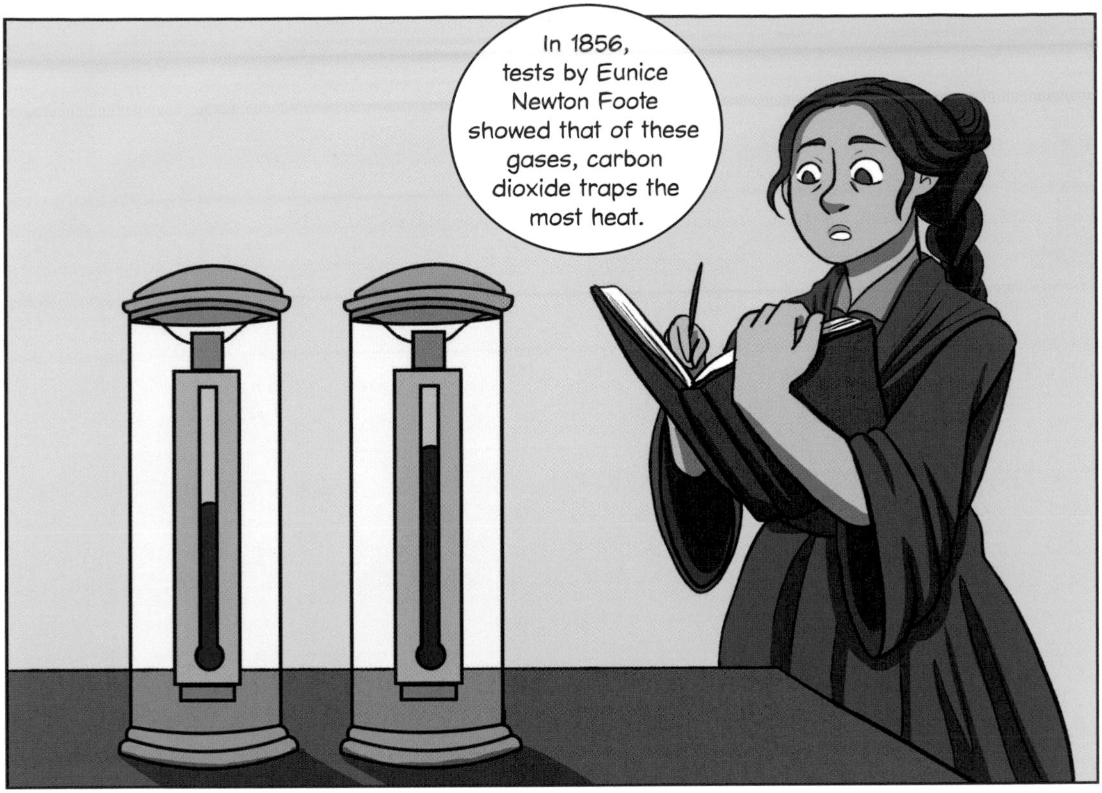
In 1856, tests by Eunice Newton Foote showed that of these gases, carbon dioxide traps the most heat.

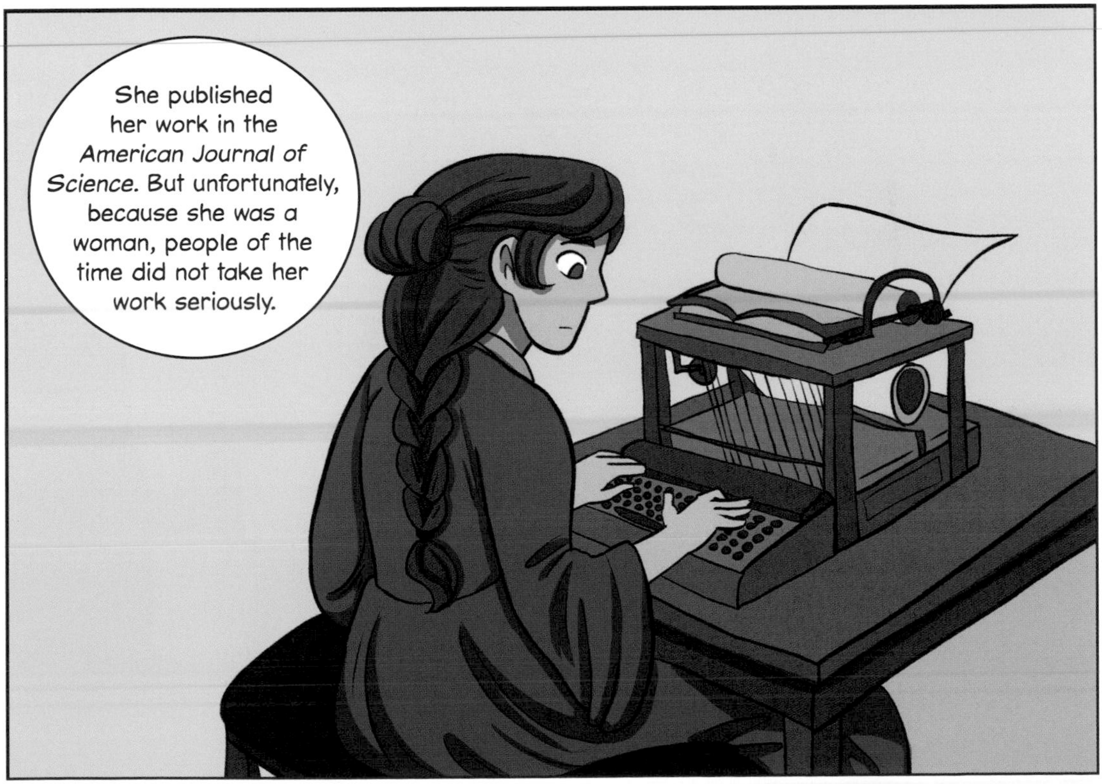
She published her work in the *American Journal of Science*. But unfortunately, because she was a woman, people of the time did not take her work seriously.

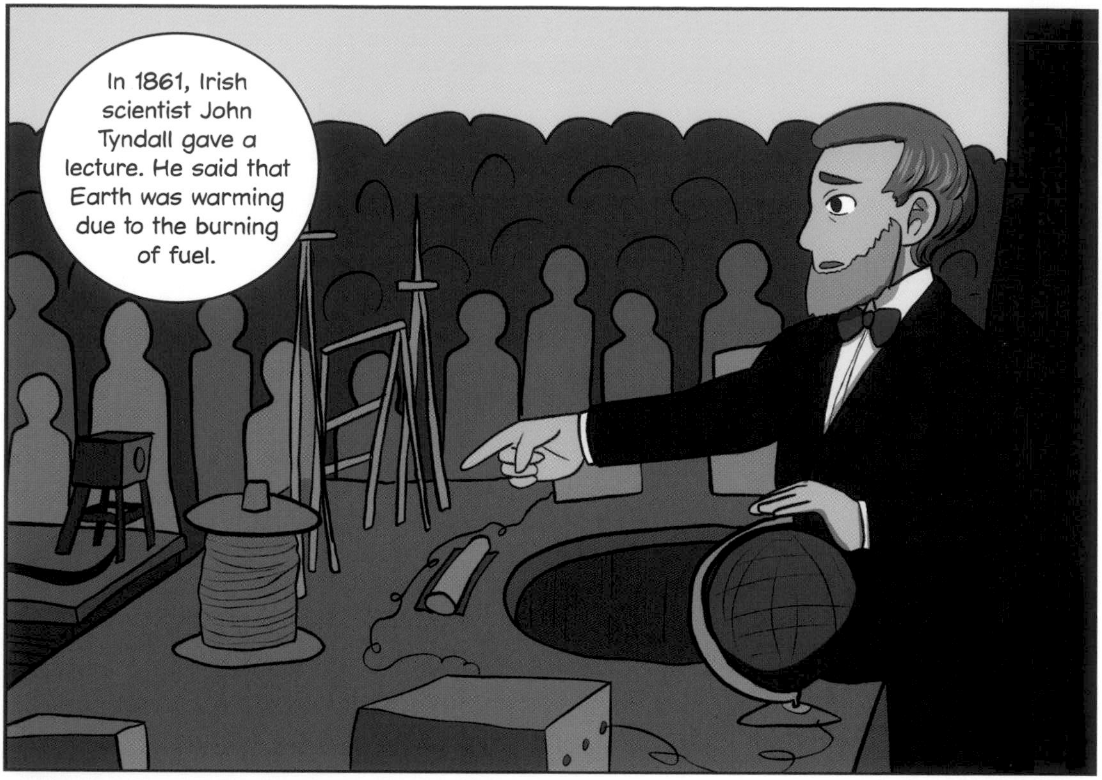
In 1861, Irish scientist John Tyndall gave a lecture. He said that Earth was warming due to the burning of fuel.

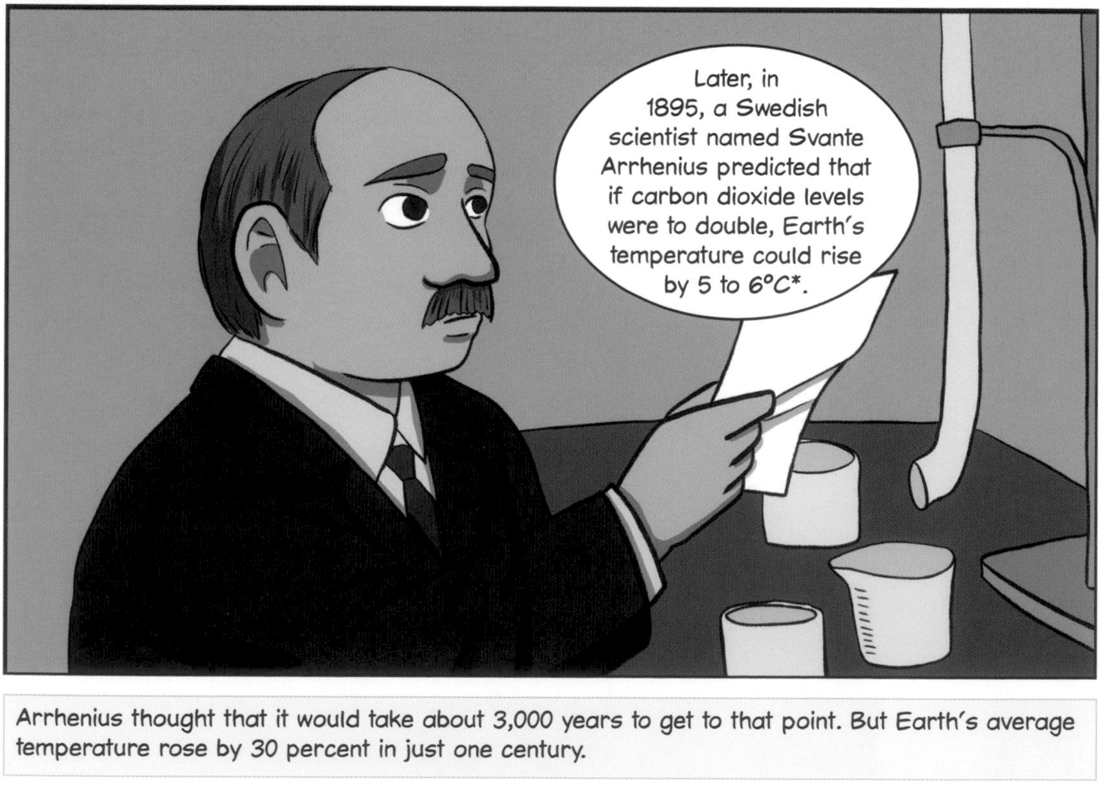
Later, in 1895, a Swedish scientist named Svante Arrhenius predicted that if carbon dioxide levels were to double, Earth's temperature could rise by 5 to 6°C*.

Arrhenius thought that it would take about 3,000 years to get to that point. But Earth's average temperature rose by 30 percent in just one century.

*9 to 10.8°F

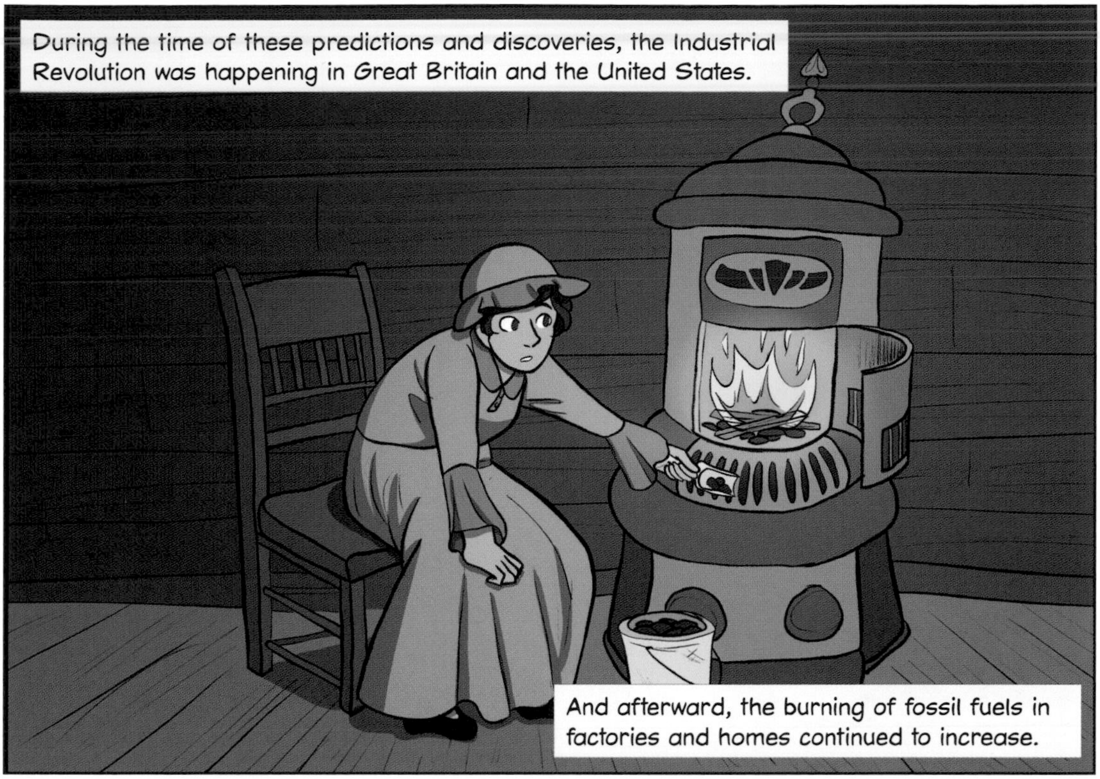
During the time of these predictions and discoveries, the Industrial Revolution was happening in Great Britain and the United States.
And afterward, the burning of fossil fuels in factories and homes continued to increase.

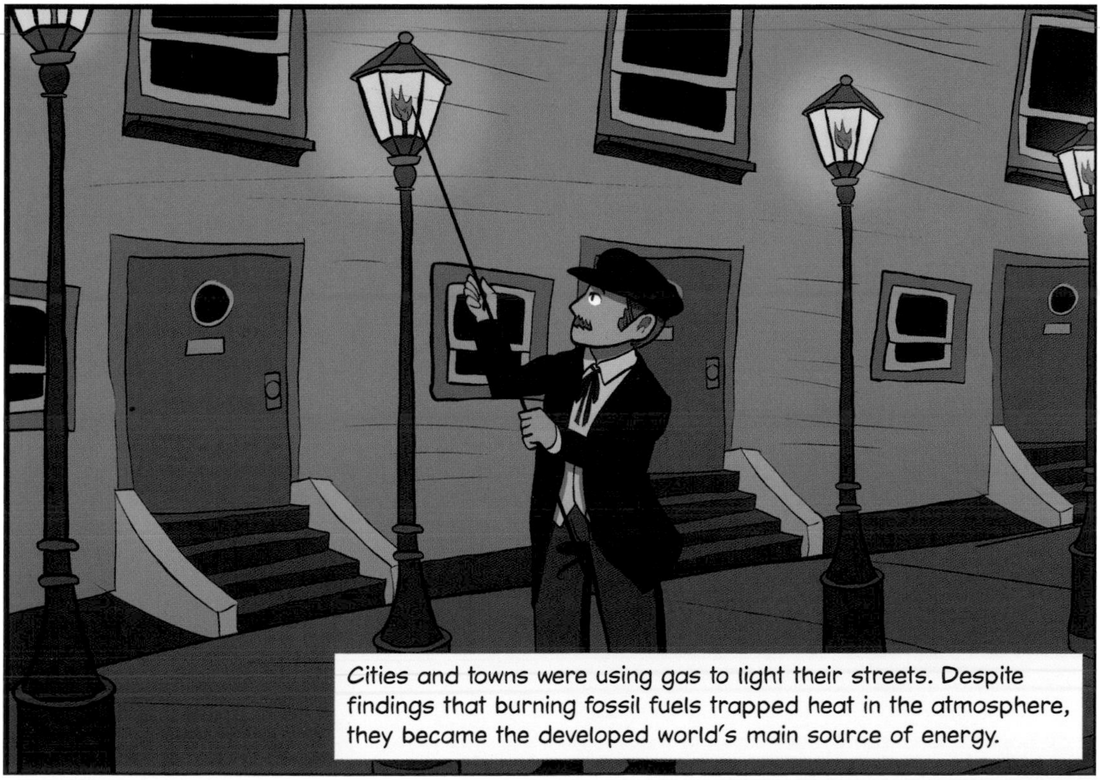
Cities and towns were using gas to light their streets. Despite findings that burning fossil fuels trapped heat in the atmosphere, they became the developed world's main source of energy.

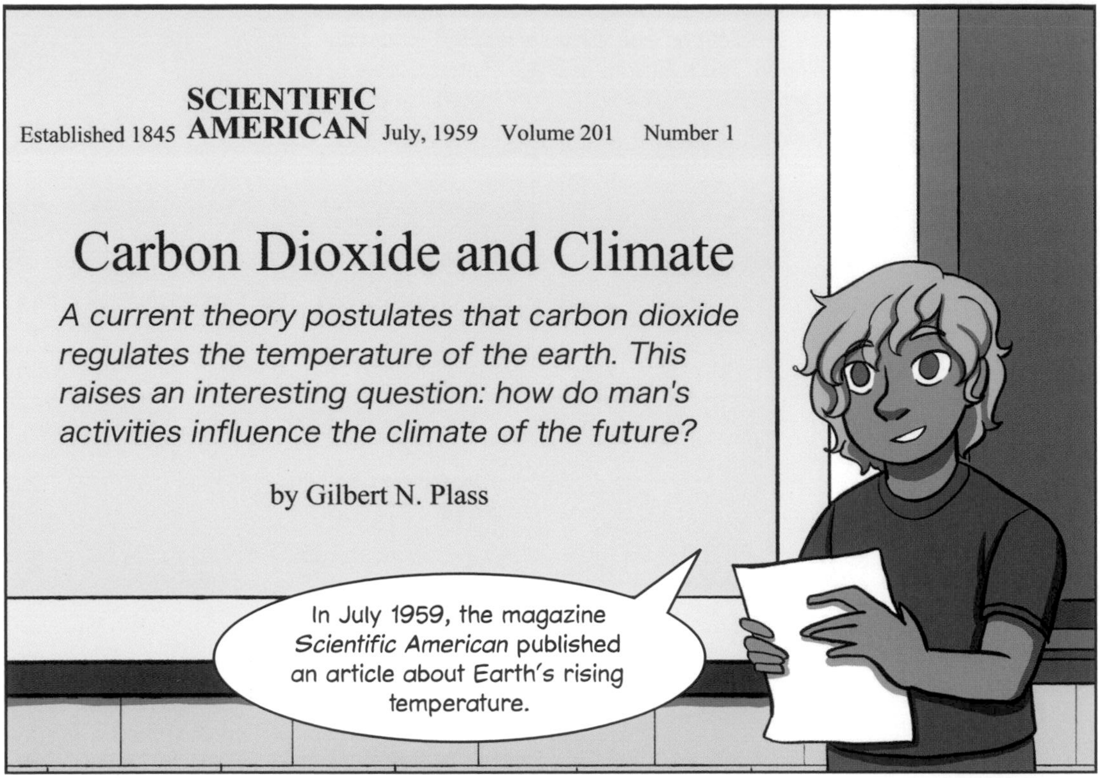
SCIENTIFIC AMERICAN
Established 1845 July, 1959 Volume 201 Number 1
Carbon Dioxide and Climate
A current theory postulates that carbon dioxide regulates the temperature of the earth. This raises an interesting question: how do man's activities influence the climate of the future?
by Gilbert N. Plass
In July 1959, the magazine *Scientific American* published an article about Earth's rising temperature.

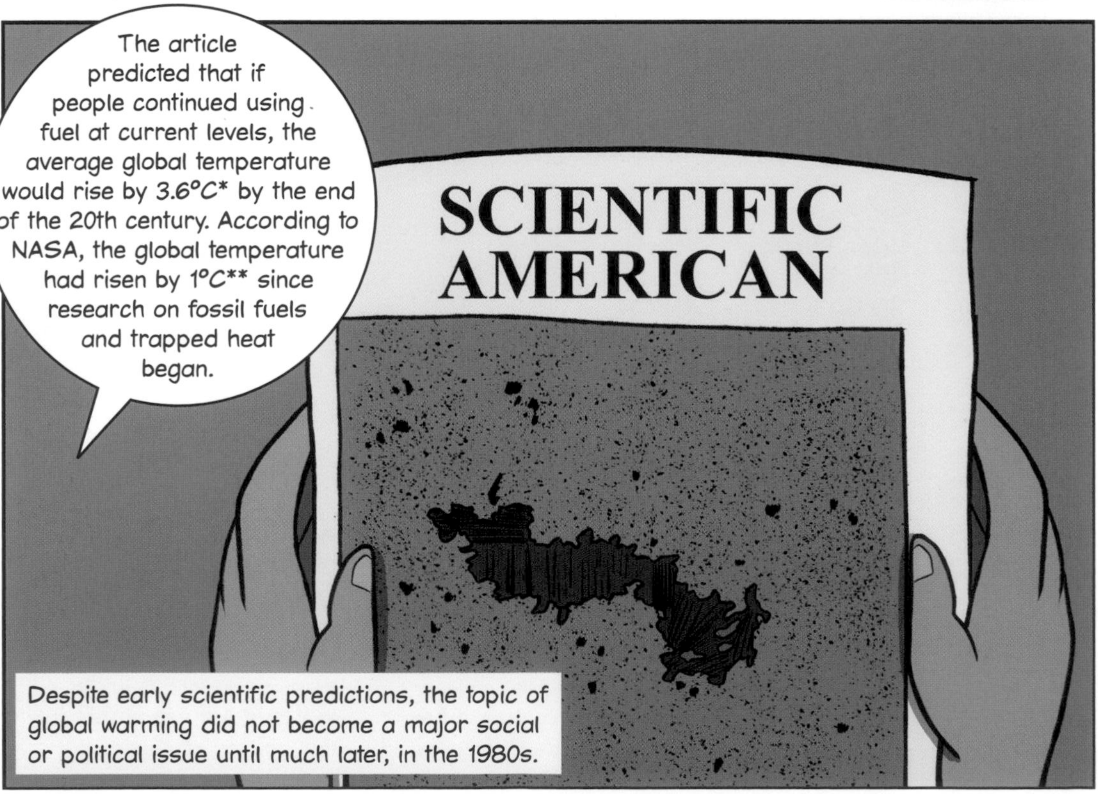
The article predicted that if people continued using fuel at current levels, the average global temperature would rise by 3.6°C* by the end of the 20th century. According to NASA, the global temperature had risen by 1°C** since research on fossil fuels and trapped heat began.
SCIENTIFIC AMERICAN
Despite early scientific predictions, the topic of global warming did not become a major social or political issue until much later, in the 1980s.

*6.5°F **1.8°F

In 1988, NASA scientist James Hansen warned the US government that fossil fuels had caused a greenhouse effect.

It is time to stop waffling so much and say that the evidence is pretty strong that the greenhouse effect is here.

The greenhouse effect has been detected, and it is changing our climate now.

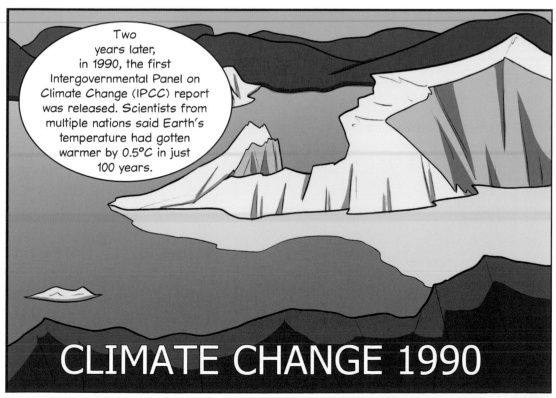

Two years later, in 1990, the first Intergovernmental Panel on Climate Change (IPCC) report was released. Scientists from multiple nations said Earth's temperature had gotten warmer by 0.5°C in just 100 years.

CLIMATE CHANGE 1990

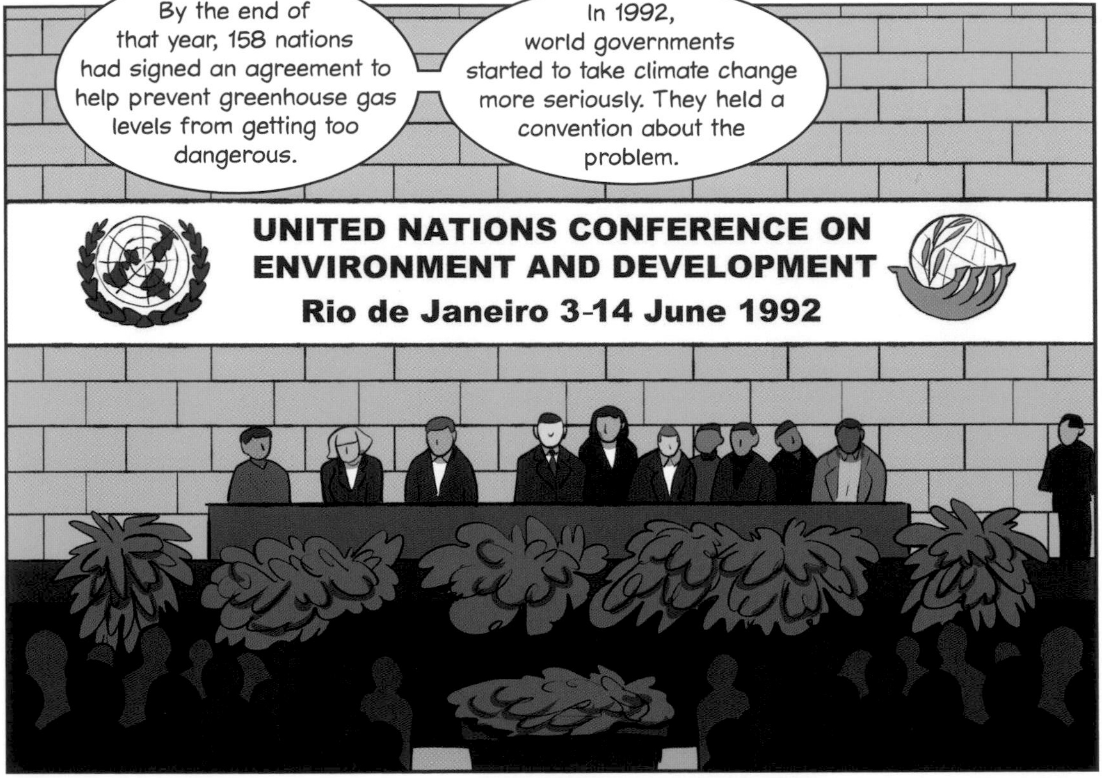
In 1992, world governments started to take climate change more seriously. They held a convention about the problem.
By the end of that year, 158 nations had signed an agreement to help prevent greenhouse gas levels from getting too dangerous.
UNITED NATIONS CONFERENCE ON ENVIRONMENT AND DEVELOPMENT
Rio de Janeiro 3-14 June 1992

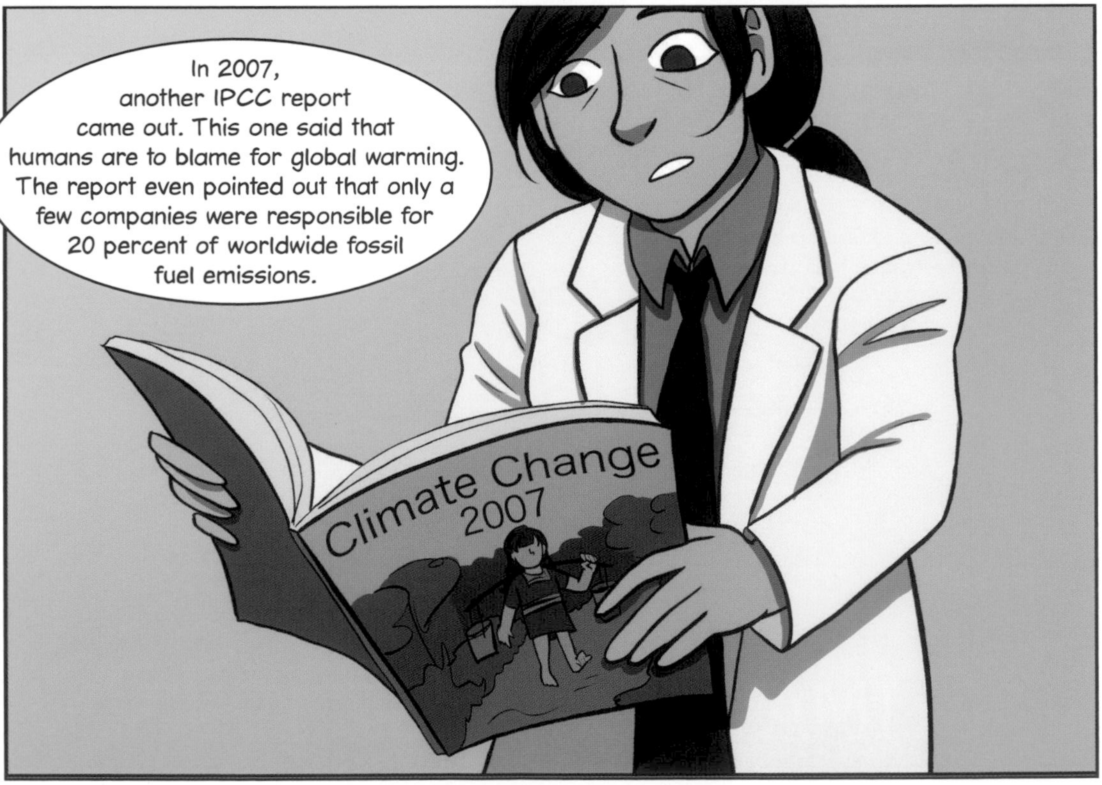
In 2007, another IPCC report came out. This one said that humans are to blame for global warming. The report even pointed out that only a few companies were responsible for 20 percent of worldwide fossil fuel emissions.
Climate Change 2007

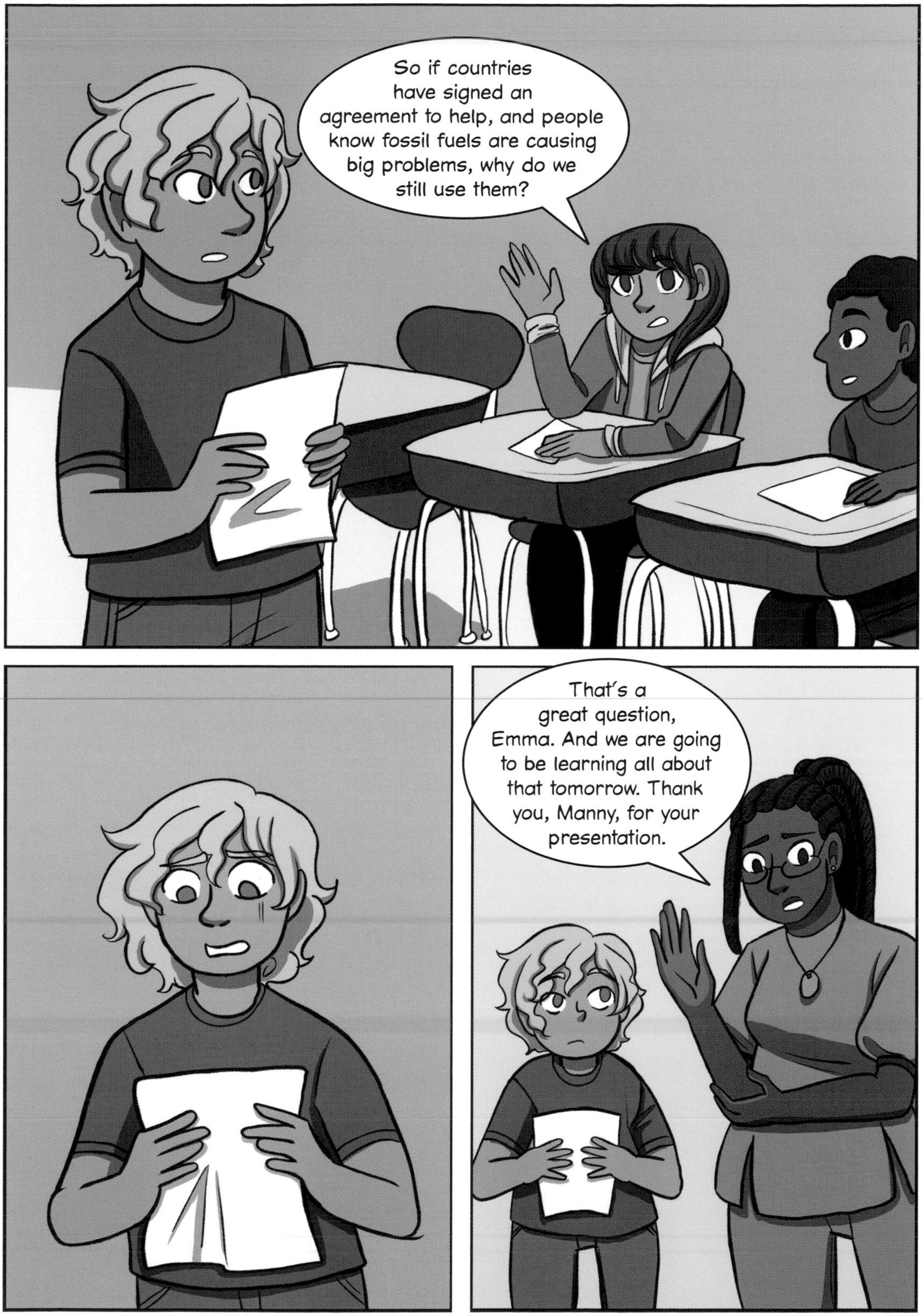
So if countries have signed an agreement to help, and people know fossil fuels are causing big problems, why do we still use them?
That's a great question, Emma. And we are going to be learning all about that tomorrow. Thank you, Manny, for your presentation.

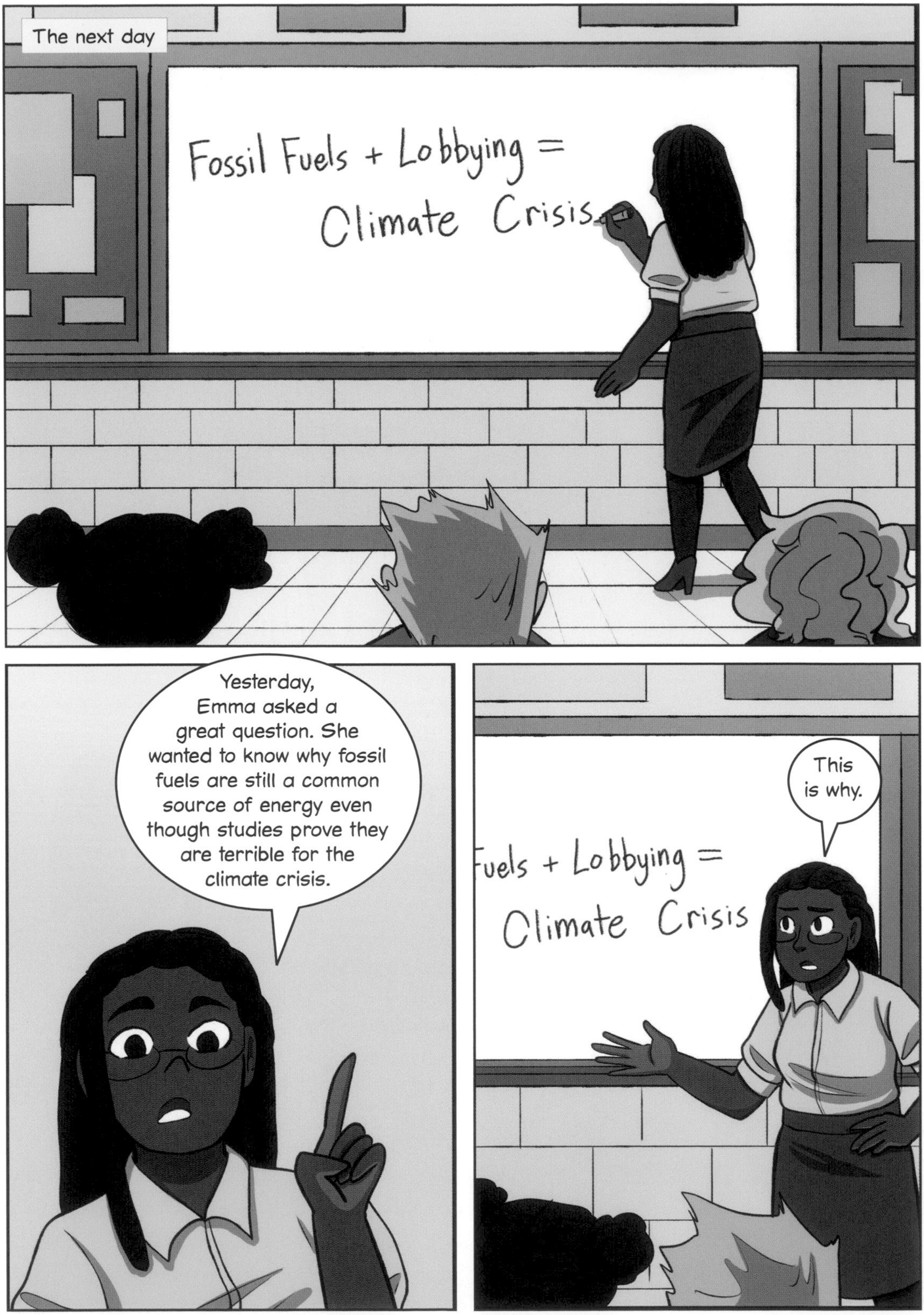

The next day
Fossil Fuels + Lobbying = Climate Crisis
Yesterday, Emma asked a great question. She wanted to know why fossil fuels are still a common source of energy even though studies prove they are terrible for the climate crisis.
Fuels + Lobbying = Climate Crisis
This is why.

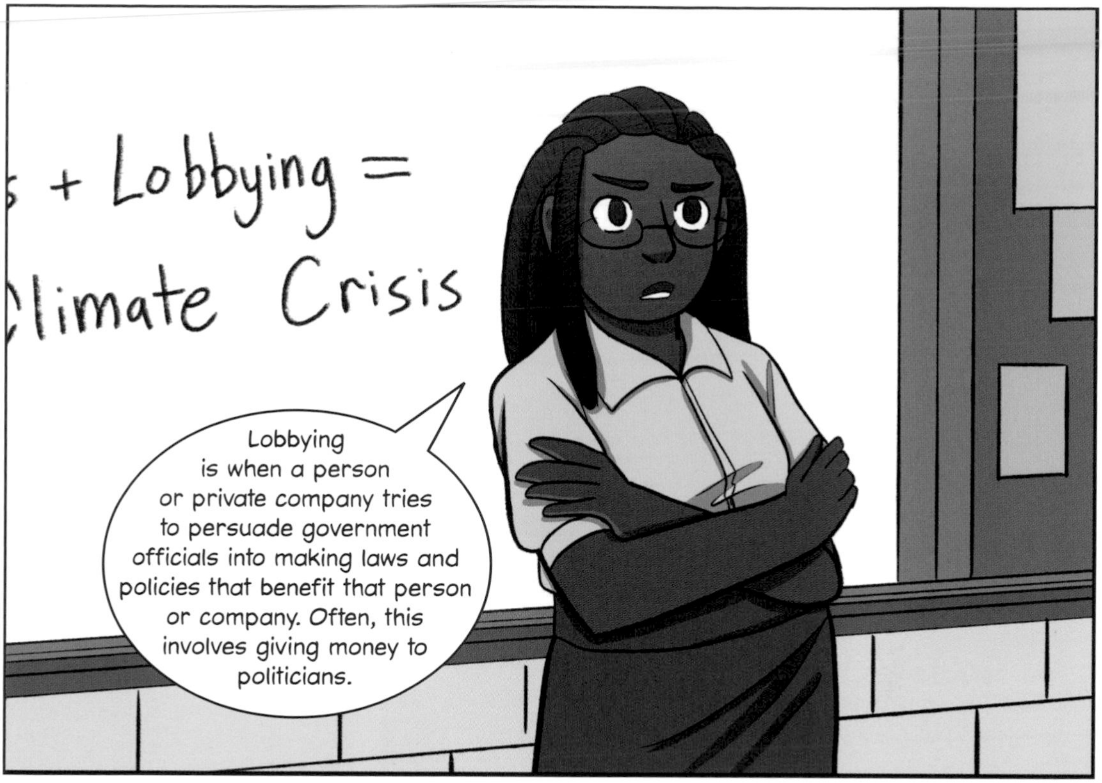
s + Lobbying =
Climate Crisis
Lobbying is when a person or private company tries to persuade government officials into making laws and policies that benefit that person or company. Often, this involves giving money to politicians.

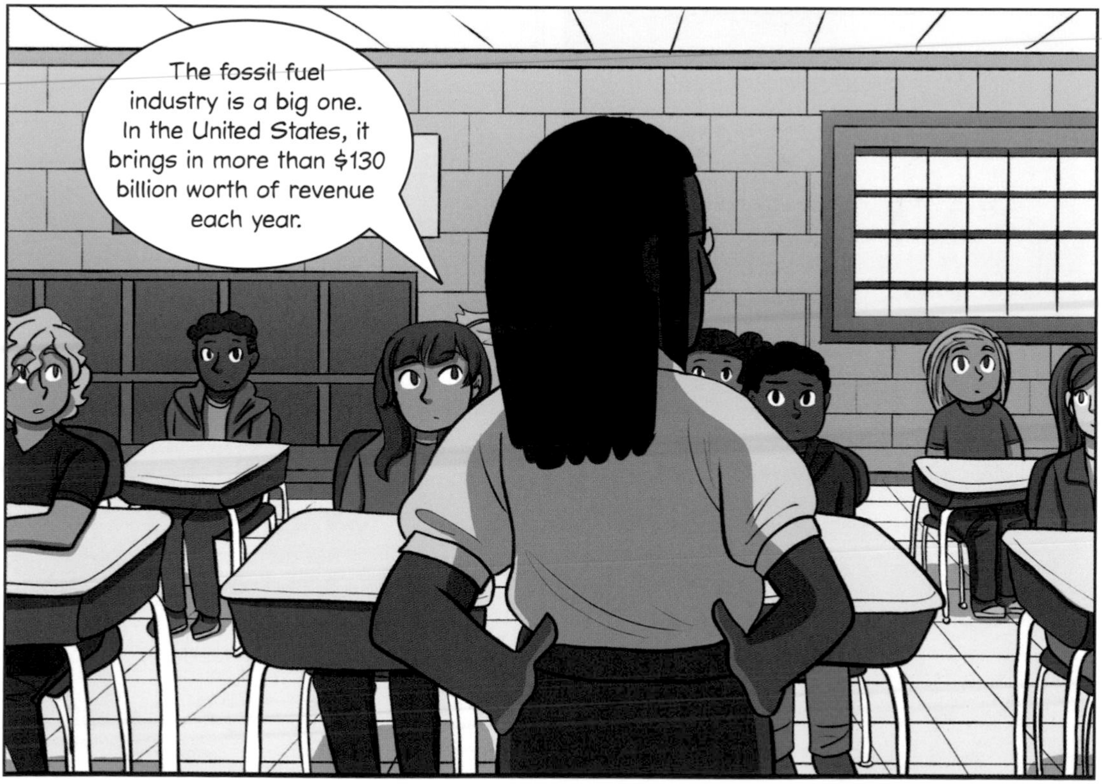
The fossil fuel industry is a big one. In the United States, it brings in more than $130 billion worth of revenue each year.

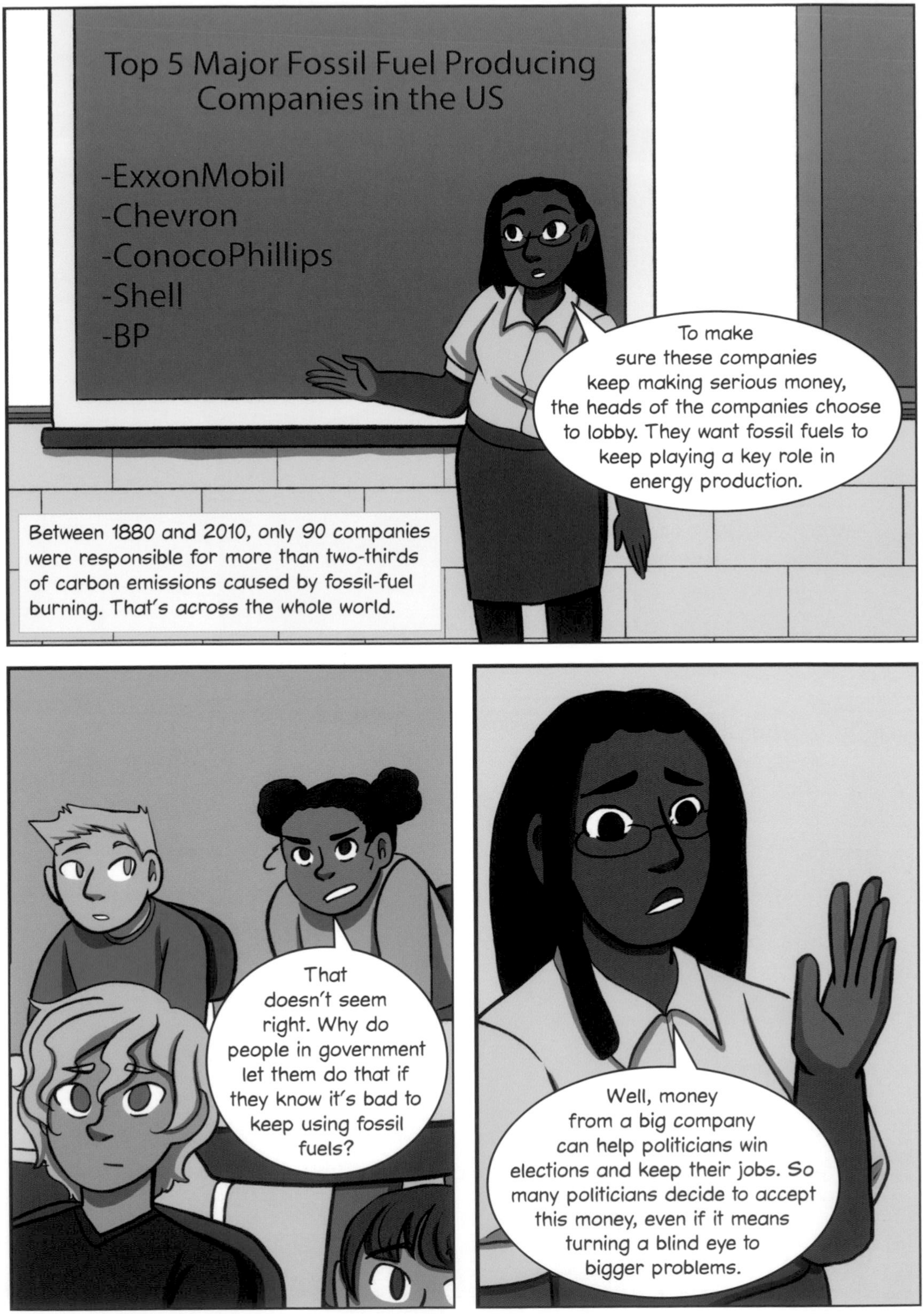

Top 5 Major Fossil Fuel Producing Companies in the US
-ExxonMobil
-Chevron
-ConocoPhillips
-Shell
-BP
To make sure these companies keep making serious money, the heads of the companies choose to lobby. They want fossil fuels to keep playing a key role in energy production.
Between 1880 and 2010, only 90 companies were responsible for more than two-thirds of carbon emissions caused by fossil-fuel burning. That's across the whole world.
That doesn't seem right. Why do people in government let them do that if they know it's bad to keep using fossil fuels?
Well, money from a big company can help politicians win elections and keep their jobs. So many politicians decide to accept this money, even if it means turning a blind eye to bigger problems.

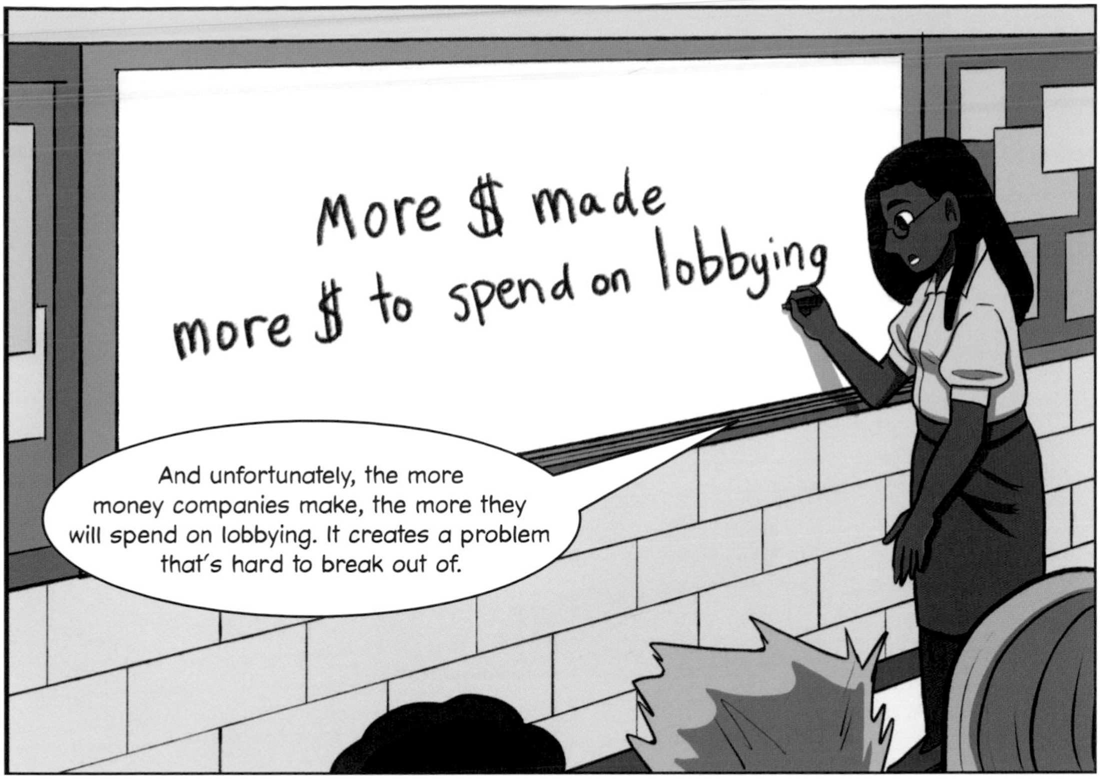
More $ made
more $ to spend on lobbying
And unfortunately, the more money companies make, the more they will spend on lobbying. It creates a problem that's hard to break out of.

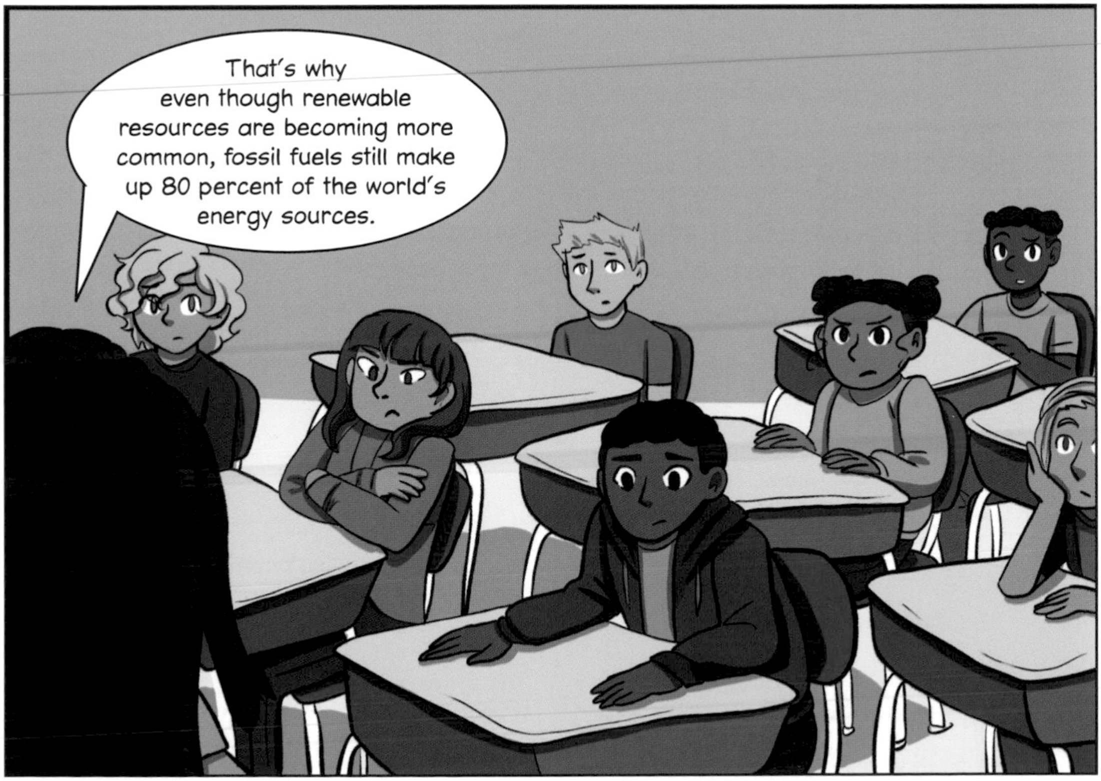
That's why even though renewable resources are becoming more common, fossil fuels still make up 80 percent of the world's energy sources.

Chapter Four: Alternatives to Fossil Fuels

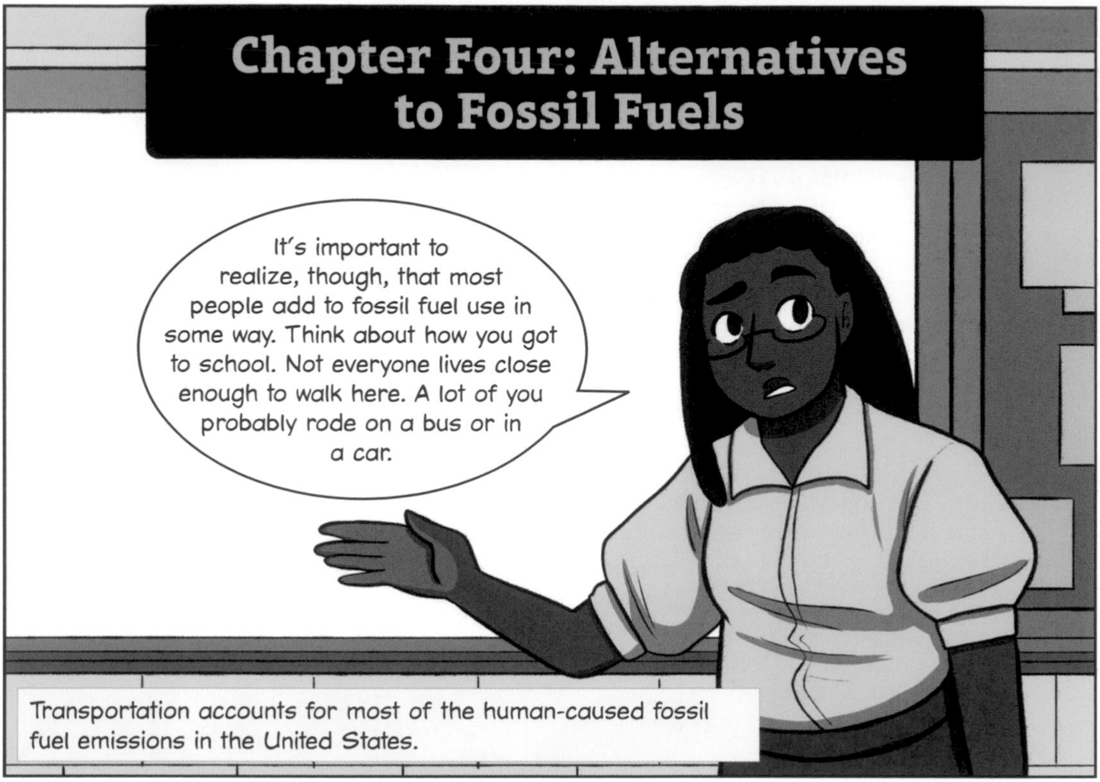
It's important to realize, though, that most people add to fossil fuel use in some way. Think about how you got to school. Not everyone lives close enough to walk here. A lot of you probably rode on a bus or in a car.
Transportation accounts for most of the human-caused fossil fuel emissions in the United States.

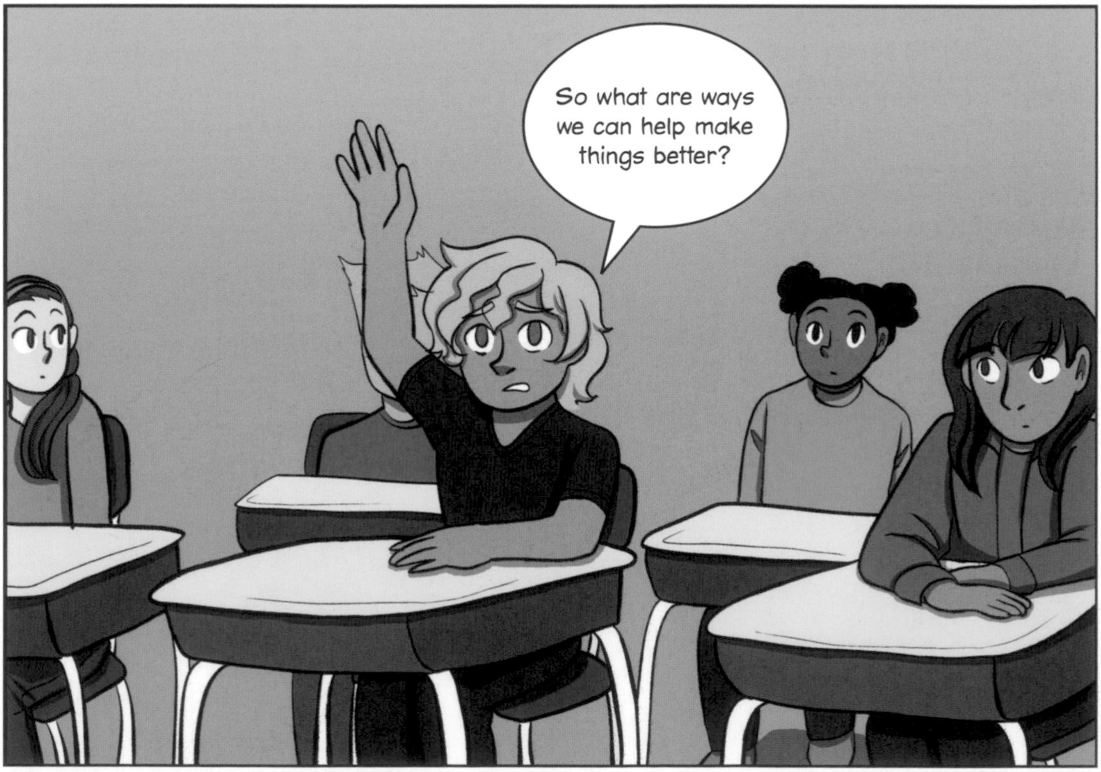
So what are ways we can help make things better?

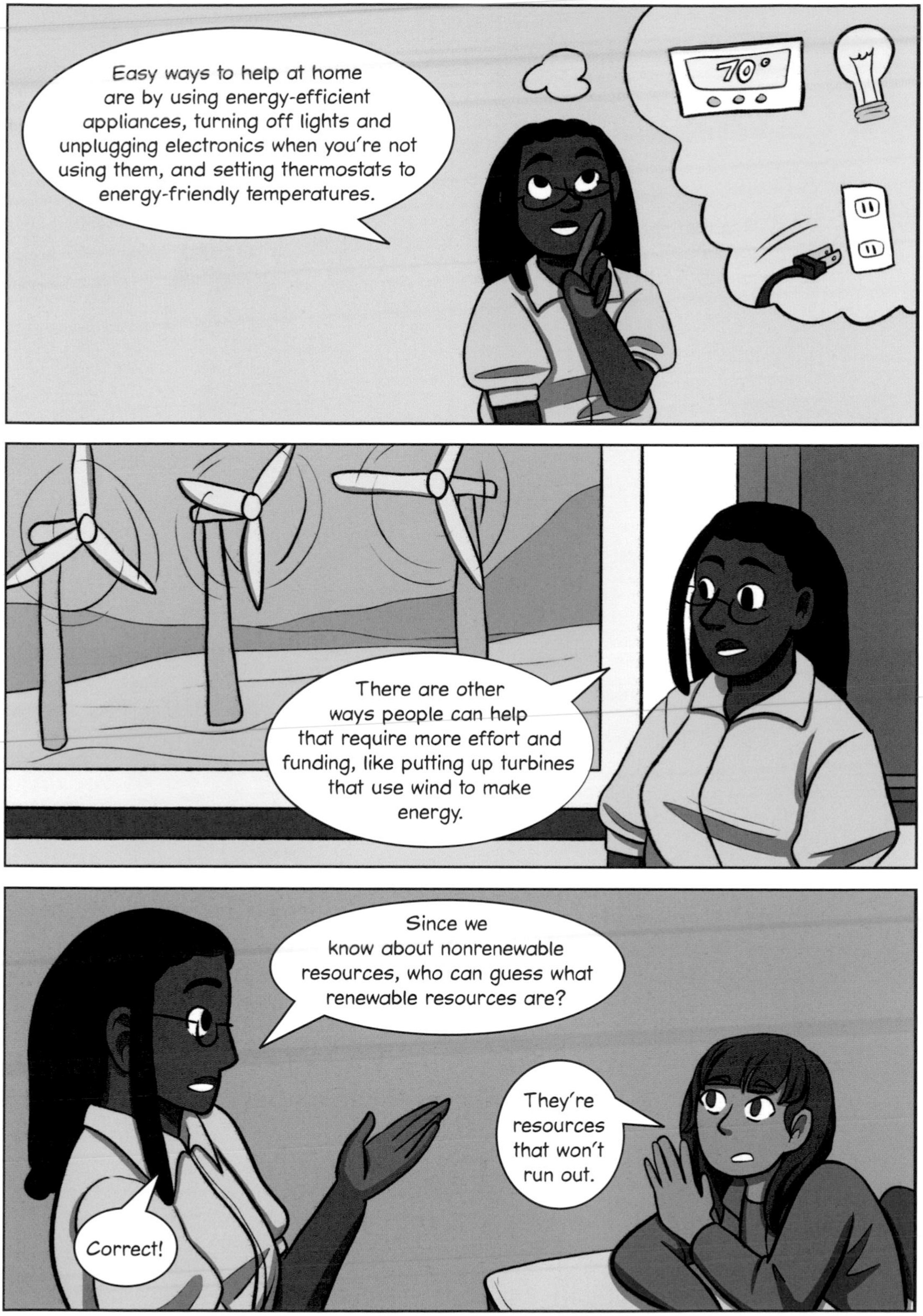
Easy ways to help at home are by using energy-efficient appliances, turning off lights and unplugging electronics when you're not using them, and setting thermostats to energy-friendly temperatures.
70°
There are other ways people can help that require more effort and funding, like putting up turbines that use wind to make energy.
Since we know about nonrenewable resources, who can guess what renewable resources are?
They're resources that won't run out.
Correct!

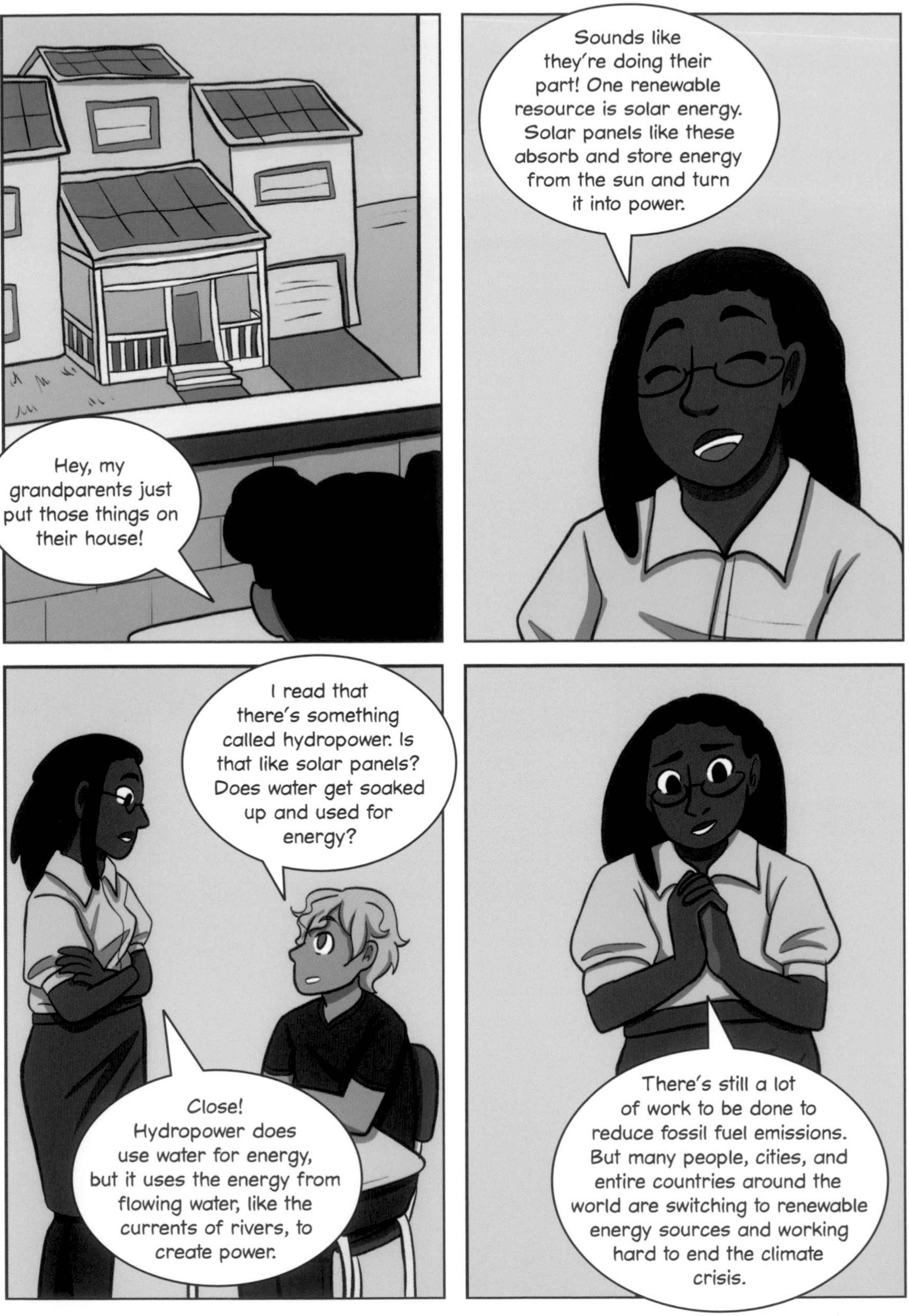
Hey, my grandparents just put those things on their house!
Sounds like they're doing their part! One renewable resource is solar energy. Solar panels like these absorb and store energy from the sun and turn it into power.
I read that there's something called hydropower. Is that like solar panels? Does water get soaked up and used for energy?
Close! Hydropower does use water for energy, but it uses the energy from flowing water, like the currents of rivers, to create power.
There's still a lot of work to be done to reduce fossil fuel emissions. But many people, cities, and entire countries around the world are switching to renewable energy sources and working hard to end the climate crisis.

SOURCE NOTES

19 Philip Shabecoff, "Global Warming Has Begun, Expert Tells Senate," *The New York Times*, June 24, 1988, https://www.nytimes.com/1988/06/24/us/global-warming-has-begun-expert-tells-senate.html

19 Jonathan Watts, Garry Blight, Lydia McMullan, Pablo Gutiérrez, "Half a Century of Dither and Denial—A Climate Crisis Timeline," *The Guardian*, October 9, 2019, https://www.theguardian.com/environment/ng-interactive/2019/oct/09/half-century-dither-denial-climate-crisis-timeline

GLOSSARY

climate change: long-term change in global temperatures

developed world: countries with a lot of industrial activity and that are economically advanced

emissions: things that are released into the air, like gas

extraction: taking or pulling out something, usually by force

fossil fuels: natural fuel formed from the remains of plants and animals

global warming: a process that causes Earth to get hotter

greenhouse effect: the sun's warmth getting trapped in the atmosphere

greenhouse gas: gas in Earth's atmosphere that traps in heat

lobbying: seeking to influence a politician or government on a specific issue

nonrenewable resources: resources that cannot be replenished once they are used up

renewable resources: resources that can naturally replenish themselves

revenue: money made by an organization or business

FURTHER READING

Climate Kids
https://www.climatekids.org/

Kehoe, Rachel. *Future Fuels to Fight Climate Change*. Lake Elmo, MN: Focus Readers, 2023.

NASA Climate Kids: The Story of Fossil Fuels
https://climatekids.nasa.gov/fossil-fuels-coal/

Rhuday-Perkovich, Olugbemisola. *Saving Earth: Climate Change and the Fight for Our Future*. New York: Farrar Straus Giroux, 2022.

INDEX